FIGHT!

HOW TRUMP AND THE MAGA MOVEMENT ARE CHANGING THE WORLD

AMERICA'S PATRIOT PROFESSOR

DR. STEVE TURLEY

Published by Turley Publishing–Lancaster, Pennsylvania

Cover photo credit: Anna Moneymaker/Getty Images
Cover design and interior layout: Chris Boyer

Printed in the United States.

ISBN: 979-8-9914793-0-1 (Softcover)
ISBN: 979-8-9914793-1-8 (eBook)

CONTENTS

INTRODUCTION

It was early Saturday evening in downtown Manhattan. My wife and I were visiting my oldest daughter who just got her first job at an international law firm in New York. We were just seated at one of the few remaining tables inside a popular local pub that was already hopping just after 6pm.

Then I got a text.

It was from my son. "Dad, you have to see what just happened to Trump!"

My heart sank. I knew it.

I knew that in mere seconds I was going to be reading about President Donald J. Trump having been shot.

My hands were shaking as I pulled up my X feed. At the top, the very first tweet I saw featured a video with the comment: "Trump was just shot on live TV! Please stop what you're doing and pray!"

I watched the video. It stopped right after he fell to the ground.

I prayed.

And then, as I continued to scroll through the frantic tweets, I saw what has now become one of the most iconic moments in American history: Trump rose to his feet, blood spilling down the side of his head, not knowing the full extent of his injuries, not knowing what would become of himself, he stood up, looked to the crowd of thousands in front of him and millions watching online, raised his hand high in the air, and shouted out:

"Fight! Fight! Fight!"

Tears welled up in my eyes. It was akin to a scene from *Braveheart*, with William Wallace rousing his disheartened countrymen to rise up and fight for their freedom. Or one of my favorite scenes from *The Two Towers*, the second of Peter Jackson's *The Lord of the Rings* trilogy, when Frodo began to despair and asked Sam what could possibly keep them going in the midst of this hell that had been unleashed on Middle Earth. "We have to keep going," Sam exhorted, "just like the heroes of old kept going; they had so many chances to turn back, but they didn't; they kept going, because they were holding on to something." "What are we holding on to Sam?" Frodo asked. Sam looked straight into his eyes: "That there's some good in this world, Mr. Frodo, and it's worth fighting for!"

In the midst of all the frenzied commentary that followed that historic day on July 13th, with all the references to that iconic moment, few in our pundit class actually asked the question, let alone answered it:

What precisely is Trump fighting for?

This book seeks to answer that question. Simply put, Trump is fighting for a new and very different world.

***

When Donald J. Trump came down his own high-rise escalator on June 16, 2015, few could have anticipated that the world would never be the same. Over the next hour, Trump would relentlessly hammer themes that characterized his campaign for the next 16 months. China was repeatedly humiliating us on trade. Mexico was laughing at us on the southern border. Globalist trade policies had decimated our manufacturing industry, and America was on the decline. It was time for Americans to rise up and take their nation back from the corrupt elite who have sold out our country for their own financial and political gain.

It was time to Make America Great Again.

In so many ways, Trump's campaign overturned what had become typical Republican talking points about lowering taxes, strengthening the military, and defeating terrorism. Those certainly were the talking points of 16 of the GOP's finest, who most political pundits believed would easily and quickly take Trump out of the running. As it turned out, it was those seasoned 16 that would end up facing their most formidable political foe.

As evidenced by the special edition published by the *National Review* entitled "Against Trump," a number of supposedly conservative intellectuals were dismissively critical of Trump's nationalist populism, as they were of Pat Buchanan's comparable campaigns in the 1990s. The self-proclaimed defenders of Reagan-inspired conservativism, from George Will to Jonah Goldberg, vociferously rejected Trump and his brash, uncouth populism. Leaders among the Religious Right openly wondered why so many conservative Christians were attracted to Trump's candidacy. For example, Russell Moore, former head of the Ethics & Religious Liberty Commission, was rather incredulous that so many Christians could support a candidate whose "often racist and sexist" language was voiced atop a career that "made millions off a casino industry" that "exploits personal vice" and "destroys families."[1]

But what eluded so many of the GOP's elite was the fact that Trump's candidacy represented a tectonic political shift that was happening on both sides of the Atlantic. Ironically, at the same time, Trump came down the escalator, the British politician Nigel Farage was leading a mass exodus out of the European Union, decrying the affront the Eurocrats in Brussels represented against Britain's national sovereignty. There were also similar calls growing in France, Italy, and the Netherlands to hold similar referenda, jeopardizing the entire EU experiment.

Since the successful Brexit referendum and Trump's

---

[1] Russell D. Moore, "Donald Trump Is Not the Moral Leader We Need," National Review, May 25, 2021, http://www.nationalreview.com/article/430119/donald-trump-russell-moore-not-moral-leader.

election in 2016, a number of scholars have recognized that Trump and the Brexit referendum were part of a wider political trend among the various nations of the world: a noticeable turn among populations towards nationalism and the politics of the populist right. While there are various reasons for this, as the following chapters will explore, this massive turn has been fueled by a collective backlash against globalism and the erosion of cultural and national identity, a backlash that few among the GOP's leadership seemed to recognize back in 2016.

Given Trump's campaign theme, Make *America* Great Again, it's understandable that so many thought the Trump phenomenon was specific to the United States. But the sentiment has clearly captured political imaginations all over the world. In 2019, as the Tories were campaigning to get Brexit done, Boris Johnson promised that he would "make Britain great again." In 2022, a book was published entitled *Making India Great Again: Learning from our History.* And more recently, Hungarian Prime Minister Viktor Orban exhorted his fellow Europeans to "Make Europe Great Again."

What precisely is this appeal? What does making

America, Britain, India, and Europe great again really mean?

Key to understanding what's happening here is something Trump began to say as his 2016 campaign began to get extraordinary traction. He said many times that this is not a campaign; It's a movement. As the media reluctantly admitted, that was certainly evident in the size of the crowds that Trump rallies routinely attracted, as well as the extraordinary engagement that Trump was getting on his social media accounts.

But as we saw with Brexit and with calls to Make Europe Great Again, this movement goes way beyond the shores of the United States. In social theory, social movements are generally defined as loosely organized campaigns made up of those who share a broadly defined common goal.

What is so fascinating is that the goals of Trump and his voters share an extraordinary resemblance to comparable goals of politicians and populations all over the world.

This book is all about Trump and this larger international phenomenon. It is an exploration of how Trump and the MAGA movement are changing the world all as worldwide dynamics are profoundly influencing Trump and the MAGA movement. I believe this reciprocity is key to understanding why Trump and the MAGA movement are just the beginning of a new and rising post-liberal world order.

The argument I will make in Chapter One is that liberalism, that political philosophy predicated on limiting executive power while maximizing individual freedom, has died, having been replaced by what scholars call *neo-feudalism*. But the key to my argument is that liberals are largely at fault for having killed their own ideology. It's not Donald Trump and the MAGA movement that are threats to liberalism, as we so often see here; the irony is that no one has undermined its foundational principles more than liberals themselves.

In Chapter Two, we will explore how the end of the liberal era has inadvertently ushered in an interim period known as *postnormal times*. The key point to understand with postnormal times is how such times dislodge populations away from an old era (what we once thought of as normal and natural) in order to bring about a yet-to-be-defined new era. The dynamics of postnormality, by definition, disrupt the old normal and anticipate a new normal. It does this by delegitimating the old normal in such a way that de-aligns populations away from old political norms, thus opening up unprecedented opportunities for new politicians advocating a new politics to take the nation in a different direction. Hence, ironically, liberals, having fatally wounded their own political ideology, only have themselves to blame for the rise of Donald Trump.

In Chapter Three, we will discover how this new politics has shaped into the rise of what scholars call *civilizational populism* in both the United States and Europe. On both sides of the Atlantic, postnormal times are contributing inordinately to a new politics that are distinctively civilizational, exemplifying uncannily common characteristics among different international populations. This political commonality results from comparable concerns over a common enemy, namely globalism and its corrupt elite. The important point here is that what is often referred to as 'Trumpism' is actually a representative symbol of a far larger and diverse international movement that is redefining the political order in multiple countries.

In Chapter Four, we will discover how this rising

civilizationalist world is upending what's called the liberal international order, along with Trump's role in dismantling that order. We'll see, in particular, how Trump is part of a global transition away from a *unipolar* world toward a rising *multipolar* world, and the dynamics behind this transition.

In Chapter Five, we will look at the rise of what is commonly referred to as a *parallel economy*,, which largely began with the cancellation of Trump from Twitter and Facebook, and has contributed to a highly polarized political economy. However, we will find that the dynamics propelling a parallel economy in America actually parallel a much larger alternative economy rising in the East, at the behest, particularly of Russia and China, an international economy that already appears to be surpassing that of Western powers.

The overall argument I want to advance is that Donald Trump and the MAGA movement are part of a much larger worldwide political paradigm shift, a shift that Trump and MAGA have both shaped and have been shaped by, that is indelibly transforming the international political and economic order. It is a tectonic shift that shows no signs of dissipating, regardless of what happens in our presidential election in November. The question is simply the extent to which the American electorate wants to participate in such an extraordinary and inevitable transition.

As such, Trump and the MAGA movement are not merely changing America; they are, in a very real and unstoppable way, changing the world.

CHAPTER ONE

THE DAY LIBERALISM DIED

November 8, 2016: a political earthquake sent shock-waves around the world. For the very first time in American history, a candidate with no prior political or military experience won the presidential election. And he didn't just win; with the implosion of the Democrat Blue Wall (a collection of three heavily blue-collar states: Pennsylvania, Wisconsin, and Michigan), he was the first Republican to garner over 300 electoral votes since 1988.

The shocked expression that collectively riddled the faces of our pundit class that night was the stuff of legend. For months leading up to that moment, they had convinced themselves that for at least the next four years, they would be referring to the commander-in-chief as Madame President. As it turned out, that would be Madame President was so electorally humiliated that she couldn't even bring herself to deliver her pained concession speech until well into the following day.

If we were to believe the shocked hysterics of the legacy media, November 8, 2016, was the day democracy died. Donald Trump, who ran on the promise of dismantling the liberal globalist order and restoring national sovereignty, to Make America Great Again, was decried unanimously by our petty pundit class as representing the single greatest threat to our liberal democratic way of life.

And yet, in retrospect, little did we know at the time that our constitutional republic was indeed imperiled, but as it turns out, that threat was not from Donald Trump; the threat was from the supposed proponents and guardians of liberalism itself.

AN INEVITABLE DEMISE

It is widely acknowledged that the United States, founded upon the principles of life, liberty, and the pursuit of happiness, largely embodied the essence of classical liberal ideals. Inspired by the writings of liberal philosophers such as John Locke, Jean-Jacques Rousseau, and John Stuart Mill, the nation's founding fathers envisioned a society where individuals could freely express their opinions, pursue their aspirations, and live free from arbitrary authority. This vision, deeply ingrained in the fabric of American society serves as a testament to the enduring legacy of liberalism and its profound impact on the nation's history and identity.

Liberalism traces its roots to the 16th and 17th centuries, when the term *liberal* initially emerged, albeit with negative connotations, in English discourse. Derived from the Latin word liberalis, meaning "befitting a free person," its early usage connoted a sense of emancipation from constraints in speech or action. However, it wasn't until the Age of the Enlightenment in the 18th century that liberalism underwent a transformative evolution, emerging as a distinct political philosophy advocating for many of the principles that established the West as a powerhouse—from representative democracy to the rule of law and equality under the law.

This transformation happened largely through what epistemologists consider a genuine revolution in knowledge. In other words, the 18th century was successful in redefining our politics because it first redefined how we came to know the world around us. Enlightenment philosophers increasingly began to view knowledge as limited solely to that which could be verified by a method, namely, the application of science and mathematics. It was argued that only those things that could be verified by the empirical method were those things that could be known in a way that was completely detached from the preconceptions of the observer. Anything that was not subjected to or failed this method, most particularly religion and religious belief, was reduced to the state of subjectivity and person-relativity and excluded from the arena of what can be known.

The argument for the primacy of the scientific method for knowledge was that knowledge was now open to everyone: all anyone had to do, in any area of knowledge, was to apply the scientific method. Thus, this highly democratic conception of knowledge buttressed democratic sentiments as a whole. According to Sally Engle Merry, we first begin seeing science and statistics cited in Europe during the 1820s and 1830s, and by the mid-nineteenth century, the French began to see scientific knowledge as indispensable to the very transparency necessary for a functioning democracy.[2] It's no wonder that rationality appears to be one of Michael Freeden's seven core concepts of liberal thought.[3]

And yet, the promise of scientific rationalism to secure both unbridled political freedoms along with technological advancement met with a rather untimely and abrupt demise. The dissolution appears rooted in the scientific method itself, namely, its reliance on the role of doubt. It's widely recognized that scientific rationalism is rooted in doubt and skepticism, which is supposedly dispelled by the application of the scientific method itself. In the pursuit of truth, one must, in good Cartesian fashion, doubt everything until one finds that which can no longer be doubted.

And yet, it has long been recognized that such doubt

---

[2] S.E. Merry, "Measuring the World: Indicators, Human Rights, and Global Governance," in Ruth Buchan, et al (eds.) *Law in Transition: Human Rights, Development and Transitional Justice* (Oxford: Hart Publishing, 2014), 141-65.

[3] M. Freeden, "The Family of Liberalism: A Morphological Analysis," in J. Meadowcroft (ed.), *The Liberal Political Tradition: Contemporary Reappraisals* (London: Edward Elgar, 1996), 14–39.

and skepticism intrinsic to modern knowledge is inherently self-negating in that such doubt and skepticism could just as easily be applied to modern epistemology itself. That's precisely what happened in the universities in the 1960s when a number of disciplines in the academy began to doubt the existence of objective truth because they discovered that there was an infinite number of ways of perceiving the world. Psychologists found that there were innumerable possible perceptions of reality, all the while literary critics realized that there was no objective interpretation of a written text. In addition, sociologists and cultural anthropologists had been long arguing that knowledge itself is largely a social construct, and there are, in point of fact, a myriad of ways of knowing the world depending on the culture constructing the knowledge.

By the 1970s, French sociologist Francois Lyotard found that such skepticism went mainstream, with the vast majority of Western populations rejecting the scientific rationalist metanarrative.[4] There appear to

---

[4] Jean-François Lyotard, *The Postmodern Condition: A Report on Knowledge* (Manchester: Manchester University Press, 1979).

be a number of reasons for this widespread rejection of modern knowledge: the disillusionment from the World Wars; the rise of global communism; the counter-culture movements of the '60s which carried modernist skepticism to its logical outworking; the increasingly pluralist nature of society with the high degrees of immigration and multiple-belief-systems starting in the 1960s; all of this just crushed that fundamental tenet of modernity that scientific rationalism was the one true way of understanding reality. Ironically, it was self-professed liberals in the academy who were the ones originally responsible for undermining liberalism's epistemological foundations.

But liberalism's epistemological demise represented only half the ruin. The other half involves the loss of liberalism's vision of individual freedom. Michael Freeden's core concepts of liberal thought highlight how liberalism, in its basic form, involves the limitation of executive power in order to maximize individual freedom. But if Patrick Deneen's critique of liberalism passes scrutiny, the limitation of executive power and the maximizing of individual freedom turn out to be mutually exclusive.[5] For Deneen, liberalism reimagines the human person as a sovereign individual who has no moral obligations apart from that which he or she chooses for themselves. In the name of maximizing individual freedom, liberalism ended up eroding the intermediary institutions like family, church, and community that were historically considered necessary for a stable and flourishing society. Absent any mediating institutions, government fills the social vacuum, thus rendering the maximization of individual freedom ultimately incompatible with limited government.

THE COLLAPSE OF LIBERALISM AND THE RISE OF NEO-FEUDALISM

Liberalism's incompatibility with the limited government it claimed to restrain and the scientific rationalism it purported to uphold, has resulted in a radically ironic twist: modern liberalism has largely transformed into the very illiberal tyranny its proponents originally purported to replace. And that's not an exaggeration.

---

[5] Patrick Deneen, *Why Liberalism Failed* (New Haven: Yale University Press, 2019).

Ironically, the social world modern liberalism is creating is more akin to its feudalist precursor than anything even remotely progressive. Indeed, liberal dynamics are even now forging what scholars such as Joel Kotkin of Chapman University profoundly describes as neo-feudalism.[6] It's a term that refers to the ways in which the structure of our society is increasingly reflecting the kind of social caste system that characterized the feudal Middle Ages. For example, today, like then, there is an astonishing concentration of wealth and power, where very few people control pretty much everything. Five years ago, about 400 billionaires owned half of the world's assets; today, that number has dropped to just 100.

But next to that, we're seeing today the rise of a comparable kind of religious fundamentalism, but of course, the fundamentalism we see today is in the insidious form of what is technically referred to as cultural socialism, what we more commonly call 'wokeness.' Political

---

[6]Joel Kotkin, "Our Neo-Feudal Future: Joel Kotkin," First Things, January 1, 2022, https://www.firstthings.com/article/2022/01/our-neo-feudal-future.

scholar Eric Kaufmann sees cultural socialism or wokeness as comprised of a twofold framework: first, cultural socialists believe that historically marginalized groups (those marginalized because of their race, gender, sexuality, etc.), should have equal outcomes in order for our society to be considered just and equitable.[7] This is a commitment to what's known as *equity,* an equality of outcome as opposed to opportunity. So whether that's marriage, career opportunities, or the like, equity, the equality of outcome, needs to be the overall concern for a just society.

Secondly, cultural socialists believe that those who have been marginalized and oppressed have been excluded not by an economic system, as the class-conscious Marxists of old would argue, but rather by cultural norms, narratives, and symbols. This means that the words we use, the way history is taught in our classrooms, the way we organize the calendar and the holidays we celebrate, these are all subtle means by which we intentionally or unintentionally discriminate against

---

[7] Eric Kaufmann, "Two Roads to Woke," Law and Liberty, September 19, 2023, https://lawliberty.org/book-review/two-roads-to-woke/.

and disenfranchise these groups. And justice requires that we redefine things like the calendar (such as Pride Month in June) and how we teach history (such as critical race theory) and sexual relationality in our schools (such as trans bathroom policies) in order to include these otherwise disenfranchised groups.

However, even if we were to grant the most genuine of intentions among its proponents, wokeness or cultural socialism has miserably failed in its supposed attempt at eradicating discrimination. As Kaufmann notes, wokeness in effect sanctifies, it makes sacred, these historically marginalized groups, which in turn forms a new kind of caste system akin to the neo-feudalism we explored in our first chapter, where these sanctified groups are given special rights and privileges, all the while the supposedly historically oppressor groups (namely white heterosexual men) are subject to incessant stigmatization, being constantly accused of racism, patriarchy, cis-sexism, and the like. So today, disparaging and derogatory things are openly said about, say, white Christian men, that could not possibly be said openly about any other identity group. So inexorably, far from solving discrimination or oppression, cultural socialism simply inverts it and replaces one exclusionary caste system for another, and is thereby guilty of perpetuating the very injustice it purportedly resolves.

Returning to our neo-feudalist paradigm, there is a key difference between wokeness and the religious fundamentalism of the Middle Ages. While the fundamentalism of old was enforced by a clerical class, this new form of woke fundamentalism is enforced by a clerisy class, a class of pseudo-intellectuals from the universities and professions, the credentialed class, the so-called 'experts' who are imposing an ideological inquisition on the whole of the population. And like with all forms of religious fundamentalism, the key characteristic of wokeness is the total and complete intolerance of any and all forms of dissent. Dissenters are heretics, and heretics must be, by definition, excommunicated, hence the role of cancel culture.

Interestingly, the demise of liberalism was foreseen decades earlier by the Oxford scholar C.S. Lewis in his 1943 work *The Abolition of Man*.[8] Lewis draws out the logic of the premises of a secularized society, which

---

[8] C.S. Lewis, *The Abolition of Man* (New York: Simon & Schuster, 1975).

he sees as one dedicated to defining social and cultural progress in thoroughly scientific and technological terms. What Lewis noticed was that such a society would be comprised of two main classes of people, what he called the 'conditioner' class and the 'conditioned' class. Because the modern secular age operates according to complex technological and scientific processes, it requires a class of experts and engineers who have the specialized competency and expertise to govern this technocracy. And so, within such a modern matrix, the wider population is conditioned to believe that their health and happiness are dependent upon this ruling class of experts and engineers.

But Lewis also recognized that secular technology-based societies inevitably reject traditional moral conceptions of life. This is because technology is organized and governed by modern scientific processes, which are considered value-neutral and thus devoid of moral frames of reference. And so, with these moral frames of reference, the only way there can be a moral consensus in society is through some kind of manipulation. If a sense of divine obligation and, hence, a collective self-government has been erased, then only coercion, compulsion, and extortion can provide a motivation for ethical conformity. Thus, manipulation is at the heart of this brave new world to which we are embarking. And if manipulation is an intrinsic characteristic of modern life, then there must surface by definition two classes of people: manipulators and manipulatees, or, in Lewis' terms, the 'conditioners' and the 'conditioned.' The commitment to technological progress on the one hand and the need for coercion and manipulation in order to bring about moral conformity in an amoral world on the other, thus give rise to the formation of a social elite, a secular aristocracy, with the vast majority of the human population repositioned as objects of manipulation.

The reason why the mass population goes along with this class division of conditioner and conditioned is because the masses have been conditioned to believe that it is this class of elite experts who maintain the social conditions necessary for our health and happiness. So this class division is just a small toll that we pay for all of these wonderful benefits of living in a modern society.

In retrospect, Lewis was uncannily circumspect in his

assessment. Liberalism, in its present tyrannical and irrational neo-feudalist form, is highly illiberal. And it is precisely these neo-feudalized tendencies that came to the fore on November 8, 2016.

A NEW CORPORATE-STATE ALLIANCE

Over the last several years, we've been learning more and more just how panicked permanent Washington really was on that night. And in fairness, we have to remember that November 8th was actually the second political earthquake to stun the world's ruling elite. Just a few months earlier, in June of that year, more Brits came out to vote to leave the European Union than had ever voted for any party in their nation's history. With back-to-back victories of Brexit and Trump, the powers-that-be suddenly realized, to their horror, that these persistent populist movements that had previously disrupted mainly regional elections were no longer mere nuisances; they were no longer fringe peripheral movements: the rising populist tide had now partly dismantled the European Union, and was, as of that November, in the process of dismantling globalism itself. We now know that something happened inside DC that night: it became widely accepted among the unelected bureaucrats who comprise permanent Washington that the consent of the governed could no longer be trusted; quite the contrary, proactive measures had to be taken to ensure that the consent of the governed could indeed be managed, coerced, and, if necessary, thwarted.

Ironically, there was already a model for such a sweeping political project of control and constraint; it was a model proposed a few decades earlier by what was then a rather obscure German mechanical engineer by the name of Klaus Schwab. In his 1970 book, Modern Enterprise Management,[9] Schwab introduced a concept that would be central to the World Economic Forum, which he founded the following year in 1971, a concept called 'Stakeholder Capitalism.'[10]

Stakeholder capitalism is generally presented as a benign system in which corporations are oriented to

---

[9] Klaus Schwab, "Stakeholder Capitalism," The World Economic Forum, accessed July 2, 2024, https://www.weforum.org/.

[10] Deborah D'Souza, "What Is Stakeholder Capitalism?," Investopedia, 2022, https://www.investopedia.com/stakeholder-capitalism-4774323.

serve the interests of the general population at large, not just their investors, because, as they say, we're all stakeholders; we all have a common interest or concern in a more just, fair, and equitable society. And to that end, bureaucrats and billionaires, corporations and states should team up to work together to forge a more sustainable society.

As it turned out, the model of stakeholder capitalism overlapped perfectly with the political and economic orchestrations thought necessary to ensure that inconvenient disruptions like Brexit and Trump would never happen again. We now know, thanks to the Twitter Files, that there emerged a public-private partnership between our national security agencies in DC together with favored corporations, most particularly Big Tech social media outlets, that formed a corporate-state hybrid that largely bypassed the kind of executive restraints otherwise guaranteed by the very constitutional democracy we were being told such a partnership was protecting.

Fact-Checkers?

On November 10, 2016, just two days after the country went to the polls, Facebook CEO Mark Zuckerberg said that the possibility of "fake news" having influenced the election was a "pretty crazy idea", but he walked back that comment soon after. By December, the tech company announced that it would begin hiring third-party fact-checkers as part of a new plan to tackle misinformation being shared online. Only days later, Facebook started rolling out new tools designed to prevent the spread of what the company called "misinformation." The term has come to be controversial ever since, with critics arguing over who should determine whether disputed information is accurate or not. It's no wonder Facebook's fact-checkers never won universal acclaim from the platform's users, either, given that the company sided with obviously left-leaning organizations like Snopes, Politifact, ABC News, and FactCheck.org.

While the participation of left-wing fact-checkers may technically be remedied or countered by the additional involvement of right-wing fact-checkers, the root of the problem may simply be the fact that these fact-checkers are political, to begin with. At another time, organizations like this may have existed with the true intention of delivering on their name: to check facts based on all the evidence and information available to them, to participate in debate during that progress, and to be as transparent and honest with the platform's users as possible. But that is not possible today.

In light of the rejection of objective truth among university faculties in the 1960s, scholars such as Mary Poovey have analyzed the social and historical processes behind the cultural construction of what she calls the 'modern fact.'[11] The modern fact is a relatively new invention, concocted with an eye toward overcoming the fallibility of subjective conjecture, preconception, and bias. As we saw above, this social construction of knowledge was inextricably linked to the emergence of a new conception of republican citizenship, where statistical 'facts' were seen as indispensable to the very transparency necessary for a functioning democracy.

However, as the anthropologist of media and communication Mark Allen Peterson notes, the media's representation of facts is just that: a *representation.*[12] In other words, the "issue is not so much whether things

---

[11] Mary Poovey, A History of the Modern Fact (Chicago: University of Chicago Press, 1998).

[12] Mark Allen Peterson, *Anthropology and Mass Communication: Myth and Media in the New Millennium* (New York: Berghahn Books, 2003).

exist in the external world...as it is one of articulation, of constructing accounts of these things...however unbiased one's reporting is, the articulation of experience in words and images...always remains a construction. Texts are inevitably made, not given or discovered."[13] He notes further that choices between words such as 'militants,' 'guerrillas,' 'freedom fighters,' rebels,' 'separatists,' 'Islamic terrorists,' or 'fake news,' are not and indeed cannot be neutral choices; each term has as Peterson notes "a different set of associated meanings that become part of the reality constructed by the text. Texts become sites of ideological struggle in which different realities are contested."[14]

Thus, 'fact-checking' itself has become a site of significant controversy in which different perceptions of reality and experiences of the world, such as globalist vs. nationalist or urban vs. rural or secular vs. traditionalist, are contested. But given the neo-feudal dynamics operative behind the scenes as these Big Tech companies, it

---

[13] Peterson, *Anthropology*, 78.

[14] Peterson, *Anthropology*, 78-9.

turns out that resolving that contestation and debate was the last thing 'fact checkers' were interested in.

THE TWITTER FILES

The Twitter Files was an investigative journalistic endeavor from multiple reporters and writers who were given access to documents from inside Twitter, Inc. The Twitter Files documented internal communications from between December 2022 and March 2023 that were made available to journalists Lee Fang, Bari Weiss, and Matt Taibbi, as well as authors Alex Berenson, David Zweig, and Michael Shellenberger by incoming CEO Elon Musk.

The release of these files, and the accompanying reports, showed us that deep state agents are literally embedded throughout Big Tech. It happens right under our fingertips every single day, and yet most people aren't aware of how extensive it has become.

Shellenberger revealed in his reporting that Twitter had become a veritable dumping ground for former FBI workers, stating that, "As of 2020, there were so many former FBI employees–'Bi alumni–working at Twitter that they had created their own private Slack channel and a crib sheet to onboard new FBI arrivals."[15]

Doesn't that make you think? This is an issue that came to the fore again with the revelation that a top FBI official by the name of Jim Baker, a former FBI lawyer who worked at Twitter, was one of the men behind efforts to bury the Hunter Biden laptop story during the final days of the 2020 election. The deep state is so embedded in Big Tech that Baker, who was actually connected to the Trump-Russia-Spygate fabrication, was, in fact, responsible for vetting Twitter documents before they reached the Twitter Files journalists. Mark Hemingway of the Federalist responded to the news of Baker's involvement with the Twitter Files releases, asking whether FBI and CIA officials are being "sheep-dipped" at Twitter and other social media companies—a reference to a tactic used in government agencies whereby

---

[15] Quoted in Brian Flood, "Twitter Files Part 7: FBI, DOJ 'discredited' information about Hunter Biden's foreign business dealings," Fox News, December 19, 2022, https://www.foxnews.com/media/twitter-files-part-7-fbi-doj-discredited-information-about-hunter-bidens-foreign-business-dealings.

individuals are "discharged" from service, only to be sent to perform undercover work elsewhere.[16]

The Twitter files also revealed how, as early as July 2020, the FBI had been giving out Top Secret security clearances for Twitter executives to give them the impression that they were being told the truth when government agencies said that Russian actors were behind the Hunter Biden laptop story. In the wake of the 2020 election, even mainstream news outlets have been forced to admit that the Hunter Biden laptop is real and that it was never in any way, shape, or form a product of Russian misinformation. The contents obtained from the laptop were authentic. The photographs and the videos of Hunter Biden were real. The emails were real. Everything was real. But Twitter executives were convinced otherwise because, at the time, the three-letter agencies were telling them so.

And to top it all off, not only was Twitter censoring information and journalists, but our tax dollars were

---

[16] Mark Hemingway, "Are FBI and CIA Agents 'Sheep Dipped' at Twitter and Other Tech Companies?" The Federalist, December 20, 2022, https://thefederalist.com/2022/12/20/are-fbi-and-cia-agents-sheep-dipped-at-twitter-and-other-tech-companies/.

paying for it! According to an associate of Jim Baker, the former FBI attorney, the FBI paid Twitter more than $3 million as part of their censorship efforts. Elon Musk admitted it, too, writing on his newly acquired social media site: "Government paid Twitter millions of dollars to censor info from the public."[17]

Is it any wonder, then, that both Facebook and Twitter banned President Donald Trump from posting on their platforms on January 6, 2021? The incident was the perfect moment for these social media groups to pounce, using Trump's alleged attempt at an "insurrection" as an excuse to prevent the leader of the free world from communicating with the country. Soon after, Facebook announced that the suspension would be indefinite. Twitter also permanently suspended Trump's account, accusing him of posing a risk of "further incitement to violence."

Since then, the neo-feudal dynamics in our nation have only gotten worse. Increasingly, we began to see corporate boardrooms deliberately and dogmatically restrain

---

[17] Elon Musk (@ElonMusk), Twitter, December 20, 2022, https://x.com/elonmusk/status/1605219914813673473?lang=en.

the freedoms of citizens, particularly the freedom of speech and information, so as to maximize centralized control over the totality of political and economic life.

The very fact that this corporate-state union could, back in January of 2021, deplatform and cancel even the sitting President of the United States sent an unmistakable message to all of us: 'You, the people, are NOT in charge, we are! The system is more powerful than you, and the system is more powerful than anyone you elect to take it down! Don't even think that you matter; the consent of the governed has been effectively replaced by the decree of the elite. We, the unelected powers-that-be, have so effectively restructured society, that an offense like Trump will never, ever happen again.'

There's just one problem. He's back, and he's stronger than ever.

CHAPTER 2

TRUMP: THE FIRST POSTNORMAL PRESIDENT

If you think the world has gone crazy, you're not alone. According to Gallup's latest Global Emotions Report, a survey of people in 121 nations found that global levels of stress, sadness, and loneliness have reached record highs.[18] In fact, the last few years have exemplified the highest levels of negative emotions among world populations since Gallup started tracking emotional health back in 2006. Among their findings, 41% of respondents claimed they experienced high levels of daily stress, and

[18] Thierry Malleret, "Gallup Research Reveals Peak Stress and Sadness Worldwide," Global Wellness Institute, July 12, 2022.

positive feelings, such as laughing or being well-rested, hit record lows. It appears that everyone is experiencing it. Even those not paying close attention to world events perceive that things are increasingly unstable and incomprehensible.

Think about it: who would ever have imagined just a decade ago that Democrats would actually end up aligning themselves with the likes of George W. Bush and John Bolton, the very political figures the left spent years universally denouncing as the epitome of evil? But that's exactly what happened. Even the likes of Dick and Liz Cheney ended up becoming the darlings of far-left media outlets like MSNBC!

The reason things appear so abnormal is simple: it's because they are. That, at least, is the thesis of the British-Pakistani scholar Ziauddin Sardar.[19] Sardar argues that we are living in what he calls *postnormal times*, which refers to an intermediate period in which old orthodoxies are dying while new ones have not yet

---

[19] Ziauddin Sardar (ed.), *Emerging Epistemologies: The Changing Fabric of Knowledge in Postnormal Times*
(Herndon, VA: Centre for Postnormal Policy and Futures Studies, 2022).

been born. A post-normal time is a time of enormous transition and transformation precisely because it's an interim period between two eras: one that's coming to an end (a literal end of an era) and a new era that's beginning but has yet to establish itself. So, postnormal time refers to an interim period between a no longer and a not yet.

There are two important points to postnormality. First, a postnormal time is nothing new. We are not the first ones to live in such a time; there have been numerous generations that have lived in the interim between the end of an old era and the beginning of a new one. Postnormative analysis tries to identify what is uniquely characteristic of such interim periods so as to bring some semblance of comprehension in the midst of so much incomprehension.

Secondly, Sardar refers to this transitory period as postnormal precisely because what we've considered 'normal' in the past is now largely inapplicable in the present; past understandings and frames of reference are largely incapable of making sense of the present transitory period; in paradigm shift theory, the two periods of time are incommensurate.What that means is that we really can't rely on anything in the past to make sense of the present, because the past operated according to norms that no longer exist, in that the societal order that the past normal was indicative of is basically rotting away. So, we're in an extraordinary period of turbulence where very little makes sense.

What further complicates things is that this transition and transformation means that change is not simply happening on the surface; rather, the transformation is at the level of the basic tenets of our age's worldview. What this means is that simplistic, dismissive explanations for the turbulence of this transitory period–the very kinds of 'explanations' offered by the rather clueless pundits on MSNBC and CNN–turn out to be completely inadequate at best and misleading at worst for understanding the uniqueness of our present condition. Any account for our turbulent time must be prepared to analyze the stunning transformations at far deeper metaphysical, anthropological, epistemological, ethical, and even theological levels.

Interestingly, you would think that self-identified liberals would actually be fully supportive of our current postnormal period. After all, we're being liberated from an old era and transitioning to a new one. But ironically, liberals are steadfastly opposed to this transition. The mechanisms of power and control that they've amassed in their neo-feudal dynamics are being waged precisely to curtail and frustrate this transition.

Why?

It's precisely because, as we saw in our last chapter, our postnormal times represent nothing less than the end of the modern liberal era itself. Said differently, liberalism represents the 'no longer' wing of postnormal times, an era that an increasing number of scholars recognize has largely come to an end, as evidenced by the radically illiberal practices and sentiments of liberal regimes. Such regimes are increasingly finding themselves in the defensive position of trying to desperately cling to what remains of their dying world. So ironically, liberals today, in a postnormal society, *are the conservatives*; they are the ensconced curmudgeons; they're the ones trying desperately to prevent the change, using whatever mechanisms of control at their disposal to thwart the liberation from their own neo-feudalized and increasingly illiberal world.

Enter Donald J. Trump.

In August of 2016, Nate Silver, the wunderkind pollster who predicted the 2012 election with uncanny accuracy, argued that Donald Trump had only a 13% chance of winning the election. The prospects for such a remote victory were echoed throughout the establishment media. By November 1st, Moody Analytics predicted that Hillary would win with 332 electoral votes, which itself sparked a number of articles celebrating Clinton's inevitable coronation at the polls.

But how could the polls have been so misleading, and how could the mainstream media have been so wrong?

For a number of reasons, those offering such embarrassingly inaccurate election coverage were simply unaware of our postnormal time. The political precedents of the past that pundits and prognosticators relied on for their analysis were simply inapplicable to our transitory period of change and flux.

Henry Kissinger appears to have perceived Trump's epochal significance. In an interview with the Financial Times, Kissinger said: "I think Trump may be one of those figures in history who appears from time to time to mark the end of an era and to force it to give up its old pretenses."[20] Had members of the legacy media bothered to avail themselves of the driving forces of our postnormal times–complexity, chaos, and contradiction–the rise of Donald Trump would have made far more sense. This is because, as I aim to show in what follows, the end of the liberal order and the complexity, chaos, and contradictions that dominate our current interim period are together fostering the very social conditions that are propelling the popularity of the Trump phenomenon; hence why I refer to Trump as our first postnormal president.

COMPLEXITY AND IDENTITY POLITICS

One of the key characteristics of the end of an era is *complexity.* Because the previously reigning orthodoxy is waning, all the particulars, all the diverse, disparate elements of society that once cohered, that once held together into a coherent whole by virtue of that reigning paradigm or orthodoxy, end up splitting apart. That's

---

[20] Nicole Goodkind, "Henry Kissinger: The World Is in a 'Very, Very Grave Period' and Trump Could Mark 'End of an Era,'" Newsweek, July 20, 2018.

absolutely key to understanding our time when virtually everything appears to be shattering and breaking apart; our world is increasingly characterized not by centralization, unity, and coherence as neo-feudalized dynamics would have it, but more by tribalism, nationalism, secession, balkanization, and social fission.

This complexity is largely behind why we've seen the rise of what's commonly referred to as *identity politics*. A sample of headlines from the last few years evidences precisely this rise in both the Democrat and Republican Party. John Glynn of *The American Spectator* warns, "Identity Politics Is Killing the Democratic Party,"[21] while Perry Bacon, Jr of *FiveThirtyEight* asks whether Trump's use of identity politics is an "effective strategy" for him and the GOP.[22] The ultra-left-wing *Salon* laments the "white identity politics" of President Trump[23] all the while NPR warns that "Democrats Can't

---

[21] Identity politics is killing the Democratic Party | Realclearpolitics, accessed June 27, 2024.

[22] Perry Bacon Jr., "Is Trump's Use Of Identity Politics An Effective Strategy?," FiveThirtyEight, July 25, 2019.

[23] Chauncey DeVega, "'White Identity Politics' and White Backlash: How We Wound up with a Racist in the White House," Salon, July 17, 2019.

Avoid Identity Politics in 2020."[24] *The Intercept* claims that the "Democrats Fetishizing 'Identity Politics' Could Cost Them in 2020"[25] while *The Guardian* declares that "The Republicans are now the party of identity politics."[26]

The use of the term 'identity' is actually fairly recent, entering scholarly discourse in the 1950s. While the definition of the term remains disputed, a rudimentary definition of identity involves the constituent elements of boundedness, continuity, sameness, and difference, and recognition by self and others.[27] As applied to groups, 'identity' belongs to the same complex of ideas as 'nation,' 'nationhood,' and 'ethnicity.'[28]

The term 'identity politics' first appeared in 1979, when sociologist Renee Anspach used it to refer to

---

[24] Asma Khalid, "Democrats Can't Avoid Identity Politics in 2020," NPR, December 20, 2018.

[25] Briahna Gray, "Fetishizing 'Identity Politics' Could Cost Democrats in 2020," The Intercept, June 21, 2018.

[26] Lucia Graves, "The Republicans Are Now the Party of Identity Politics," The Guardian, January 6, 2018.

[27] Judith M. Lieu, *Christian Identity in the Jewish and Graeco-Roman World* (Oxford: Oxford University Press, 2004), 11.

[28] Lieu, *Christian Identity*, 12.

activism by people with disabilities.[29] According to the study by Mary Bernstein, the term was used only three times in scholarly journals during the 1980s, covering topics such as ethnicity in politics and status-based movements. Then, in the mid-1990s, the meaning of identity politics widened to include reference to violent ethnic conflict and nationalism.[30] Since then, the term's connotations throughout the social sciences have increased even further to denote such topics as multiculturalism, feminism, LGBT activism, separatist and secessionist movements in places like Canada and Spain, tribal conflicts in Africa, and now, most recently, nationalist developments in Europe and America.

The most breathtaking thesis for the rise of identity politics came in the 1990s from Harvard scholar Samuel Huntington and his now-class *Clash of Civilizations.* Huntington put forward a bold and far-reaching thesis: the *age of ideology* that dominated the 20th century was

---

[29] R. Anspach, "From stigma to identity politics: Political activism among the physically disabled and former mental patients," *Social Science and Medicine* 13(A) (1979): 765-73.

[30] Mary Bernstein, "Identity Politics," *Annual Review of Sociology* Vol. 31 (2005): 47-74.

being eclipsed by the *age of identity* in the 21st century. While all of the great clashes of the 20th century centered on ideology, such as the clashes between liberalism, communism, and fascism, the end of modernity spelled the end of that ideological age. Instead, populations were increasingly returning to the fundamental characteristics of identity as the basis for world organization, such as nation, culture, custom, and tradition, which meant that the global conflicts of the future would increasingly be characterized by clashes over incommensurate civilizational identities rather than clashing ideologies.

In this rising world of identities, scholars are making an important distinction between *civic* nationalism and *ethnic* nationalism.[31] While civic nationalism is characterized by polyethnic citizenship, ethnic nationalism is characterized by a more homogenous racial and cultural makeup. Given that nearly 90% of the world's states are polyethnic,[32] we can think of civic and ethnic nationalisms as kinds of *macro* and *micro* loyalties; while ethnic nationalisms involve loyalties to kin, race, and

---

[31] Ibid, 99-102.

[32] Ibid, 17.

ethnicity, civic nationalisms involve allegiances to the larger nation-state project.

This distinction explains why the political left is comprised largely of sub-national identities. I think the scholar Courtney Jung is largely right in arguing that leftist micro-identity politics generally arise from the exclusionary practices of liberal democracies.[33] For example, when liberal democracies excluded on the basis of gender, women's movements emerged; when exclusionist policies were enacted because of racial prejudices, civil rights activism emerged; when sexuality became the focus of exclusion, LGBT rights emerged, and so on. Interestingly, Carol Swain noticed back in 2002 that this collective reaction to civic exclusion was breeding a new kind of white nationalism because whites were increasingly perceiving themselves to be objects of discrimination and exclusion in terms of legitimate political expression of their ethnic concerns.[34] Because

---

[33] Courtney Jung, "Race, Ethnicity, Religion," in Robert E. Goodin and Charles Tilly (eds.), *The Oxford Handbook of Contextual Political Analysis* (Oxford & New York: Oxford University Press, 2006), 360-375.

[34] Carol M. Swain, *New White Nationalism in America: Its Challenge to Integration* (Cambridge: Cambridge University Press, 2002).

the democratic square affords opportunities for gender, ethnic, sexual, and other identity-based grievances to be expressed, identity politics appears to be an inherent part of democratic liberalism itself, organically flowing out of its occasional exclusions.

By contrast, Donald Trump appeared to have recognized or at least had a sense of the complexity of this postnormal moment and sought to articulate a uniquely unifying *macro* version of identity politics. At the heart of his MAGA slogan is a commitment to reassert our national sovereignty through strict border security, economic nationalist policies, and the revitalization of our civic and religious traditions and customs by which our diverse population could be united. Such a commitment involves unapologetically smashing the woke taboos of the politically correct guardians of neo-feudalism, all the while reaffirming our national sovereignty and unique identity as over against the borderless world of free-trade obsessed globalists and the consumer-based lifestyle values that eclipse the customs and traditions that defined our national identity for centuries.

Trump and the MAGA movement uniquely provided our nation with the opportunity to move away from fostering all of these competing and contradictory *ethnic* nationalisms and embrace, collectively, *civic* nationalism. From a civic nationalist perspective, the nation *is* a race; to be American is to belong to a national race of people. In this sense, Trump speaks to whites, blacks, Asians, and Latinos, *all* as Americans. If you read or listen to his speeches, the rhetoric of leftist identity politics and multiculturalism, which involve concerns over racial discrimination, prejudice, and disenfranchisement, is replaced with a message targeting *economic* discrimination as the result of unfair globalist trade deals, *employment* disenfranchisement in the disappearance of industrial and manufacturing jobs to a globalized division of labor, and *pay* prejudice in the driving down of wages due to mass unfettered illegal immigration. Trump deals with race but from a very different vantage point from that of the Cultural Marxist; through his vision of economic nationalism, *all* Americans are invited to benefit.

The important takeaway here is that the complexity of post-normality is breaking up the neo-feudalized dynamics of illiberal liberalism into competing forms of nationalism, which are rising all over the West, as we'll see in the next chapter. And while Trump's call to civic nationalism as over against the left's balkanized politics suffered a setback in 2020, there are no signs that the complexity behind the rise of identity politics and its competing nationalisms are going away any time soon. Trump's MAGA movement promises to remain a potent political and cultural force for the foreseeable future.

CHAOS AND THE DEATH OF THE LEGACY MEDIA

As the mainstream media's blindsided election coverage demonstrated, the complexities behind the rising civic and ethnic nationalisms have been transforming not merely the political landscape but also the world of mass media as well. This transformation is largely the result of the second characteristic of postnormal times: *chaos*.

Ziauddin Sardar sees chaos as part of the complexity in that it is yet another outworking of the loss of any coherent center by which social order had previously cohered. Because postnormal periods are characterized by a loss of common frames of reference, they also lose the logic and rationale inherent in those shared interpretive frames. It's not simply that things fail to make sense in postnormal times, but the *way* things made sense in the previous era suffers from a profound disruption as well.

For our particular postnormal period, this chaos is generally associated with the rise of digital culture and the hyperconnectivity of the internet that is radically changing how populations consume news and information. In our increasingly hyperconnected world, associations between people are not limited to time, place, or location but, in fact, extend far beyond historic frontiers, such that more and more people can communicate with anyone, anywhere, at any time.

We simply cannot emphasize enough how much the rise of a digitally hyperconnected world has changed our world, and no one is learning this more than the legacy media. For decades, the establishment media had a monopoly on the dissemination of information to the masses. It prided itself on corroborating protocols that supposedly protected the reliability and objectivity of that information. But with the rise of the internet and what scholars call the *Network Society*, all that changed. Now, the masses have access to immediate digital information by way of the web.

You'll notice that virtually one hundred percent of the initial video documentation of any significant event around the world is *not* coming from news cameras or from satellite trucks; on-the-ground, in-real-life video capturing any significant event today comes from eyewitnesses who were present at that event recording it on their smartphones! *That's* the Network Society: it's a new social order comprised of decentralized and disestablished digital information that is immediately accessed by everyone.

Now, among the wide-ranging consequences of this social hyperconnectivity is the virtual collapse of the legacy media's traditional role as the gatekeepers of public knowledge and the authoritative disseminators of information. The postnormal chaos emerges from the breakdown in the informational protocols that once supposedly separated reliable information from unreliable information. In the digitalized world of mass information, everything is basically jumbled together in such a way that completely bypasses the original gatekeeping role of the media, rendering its monopoly over information dissemination completely obsolete. Today, the legacy media is finding that they can no more control the free flow of information any more than the post office can prevent email and texting. With the same immediate access to the same information, we are witnessing what scholars call 'the death of the expert', a "Google-fueled, Wikipedia-based, blog-sodden collapse of any division between professionals and laypeople, teachers and students, doctors and patients, knowers and wonderers."[35]

More than that, scholars of Network Societies such as Jan van Dijk have noticed that people with information and communication technologies such as social media have the power to start their own relations of information and communication and spheres of influence and management.[36] Thus, they can shape their own politics and bypass the monopolistic representation of their own government's politics via established media. In other words, our age is one where the bureaucracy of old is being replaced more with what's called an *in*focracy, the rule by information.

---

[35] Liam Mayo, "Manufactured Worldviews and the Shifting Landscape of Digital Knowledge," in Sardar, *Emerging Epistemologies*, 65-83, 68.

[36] Jan van Dijk, *The Network Society* (London: Sage Publications, 2020).

And so, we live in a world today where more people own a mobile device than a toothbrush, whereas if Facebook were a country, it would have the largest population on the earth. Many of you, I'm sure, are familiar with the role social media played in the so-called Arab Spring, where protests were organized or videos of political violence were featured. In many respects, the so-called Black Lives Matter movement is a social media movement and it survives through virtual communities and conversations.

Now, the important point here is that the Network Society has provided the virtual space for the rise of not merely alternative media but new media for a new political right. And so while Fox News tapped into disaffected conservatives, those disaffected by the dominant mainstream media's liberalism, it seems that social media provided the virtual space for a mass transnational network that challenged this globalized economic and political world order that even so-called conservative Republicans were a part of. A number of articles have documented how the so-called 'Far Right' of Europe has dominated social media. And here at home, during the 2016 campaign in particular, websites such as

DrudgeReport, Breitbart News, and InfoWars received tens of millions of hits daily and billions yearly. It's no coincidence that Steve Bannon, the former head of Breitbart News, was Trump's 2016 campaign manager.

And what this neo-right network society has done is provide an alternative news world to that of the liberal mainstream media. In the aftermath of November 8th, the results of such speak for themselves. An article entitled "How Matt Drudge Won the 2016 Election" underscored the influence of the alternative media on world events, an influence that took the legacy media completely by surprise.[37] We are transitioning from an old media context that largely lectures its constituents on news events and interpretations to a new network society wherein the constituents are active participants in what constitutes a news event and its variant interpretations. An elite establishment media versus a nationalist-populist media, and in 2016, the ascent of the latter overwhelmed the decline of the former.

And of course, no one in politics had utilized social media like Donald Trump. Over the course of 12 years,

---

[37] http://www.vocativ.com/376550/drudge-won-2016-election/

Trump tweeted out upwards of 57,000 times, which included 8,000 tweets during the 2016 campaign and over 25,000 tweets during his presidency.[38] His Twitter handle @realDonaldTrump had amassed 88.9 million followers, the most of anyone in the world.

While Trump's message has been able to consistently bypass the gatekeepers of the legacy media over the years, those gatekeepers of a bygone era continue to be under the illusion that they maintain a monopoly over information. As we saw in the first chapter, both Big Media and Big Tech have come together to try to thwart the immediate access of mass data by social media users, and while they've clearly frustrated access to that information, they simply are incapable of stopping it. Again, ultimately, the powers that be are no more able to stop the free flow of digital information than the post office can interrupt email. As such, the neo-feudalized efforts of billionaires and bureaucrats are ultimately futile, which means that a new, post-liberal information age is ultimately unstoppable.

---

[38] https://apnews.com/article/twitter-donald-trump-ban-ce-a450b1f12f4ceb8984972a120018d5

CONTRADICTION AND THE GROWING CLASS DIVIDE

Along with complexity and chaos, Sardar identifies a third characteristic of postnormal times: *contradiction*, where these disparate trends of complexity and chaos move in opposing directions, creating a society comprised of radically divergent and incommensurate sectors.

Nothing demonstrated that contradiction more than the pundit class's complete misreading of the 2016 campaign. From the moment of his campaign announcement in June of 2015, not a single major media outlet took Trump seriously. Even after he did the unthinkable, taking out 16 of the GOP's finest, the legacy media complex remained steadfast in their dismissal of his chances. In the week leading up to the 2016 election, the Princeton Election Consortium concluded that Hillary Clinton had 'more than a 99% chance' of winning the presidency.[39]

---

[39] Rachael Revesz, "Survey Finds Hillary Clinton Has 'More than 99% Chance' of Winning Election over Donald Trump," The Independent, November 6, 2016.

The New York Times corroborated that assessment; on the eve of the election, they happily published the top pollster's models showing that Trump's chances of winning were anywhere from a dismal 2% to 15%. Just days before the election, CNN's Fareed Zakaria confidently predicted: "Donald Trump will lose. And he will then destroy the Republican Party."

As it turns out, the world the legacy media thought they inhabited simply didn't exist. The reality was far more complex or postnormal in our terms, and reality turned out to radically contradict the political pundit class and their mutually affirming echo chamber that bombarded the airwaves 24/7. Perhaps it was because the legacy media (rightly!) recognized that Trump was truly something different; his nationalist populism really did signify the end of an era, a political realignment that had been in the making for some time but that was largely ignored by the coastal elites that dominate the media's cultural space. But as it turns out, it was a realignment that was thoroughly in line with the kind of social contradictions inherent in a postnormal interim.

Back in 2010, pollsters Scott Rasmussen and Doug Schoen published their study on the Tea Party Movement entitled *Mad as Hell: How the Tea Party Movement Is Fundamentally Remaking Our Two-Party System*, where the authors found substantial data that showed that there was, in fact,, a major paradigm shift taking place among the American electorate, one in which the old political divides between left and right and liberal vs. conservative were dying away, and a new political divide between the people vs. the ruling class, the ruled vs. the rulers, was emerging. Increasingly, voters weren't identifying with distinct parties; they were seeing themselves increasingly alienated from an elite ruling class.

A few years later, across the pond in Britain, political scholars Matthew Goodwin and Roger Eatwell came to the same conclusion in their book *National Populism: The Revolt Against Liberal Democracy*. Their analyses of the successful Brexit referendum in June of 2016, followed by the Trump win in November, found that the old ideological divisions of Tories vs. Labor that characterized so much of 20th-century politics had actually given way to new concerns about identity, where much of the population was longing for a return to the importance of national sovereignty, cultural integrity, and the protection and celebration of our rich inheritance of our unique traditions and ways of life. Similarly, the Brexit and Trump political earthquakes were followed by a series of aftershocks that saw the toppling of leftist governments in Bulgaria, Moldova, Austria, Italy, Estonia, the Czech Republic, and Slovenia in Europe and Brazil, Columbia, Paraguay, Guatemala, and El Salvador in Latin America.

The common sentiment that these studies found on both sides of the Atlantic is a growing sense that the political class no longer represents the concerns of the vast majority of citizens. For example, between the Lyndon Johnson administration in 1964 and Barack Obama in 2012, the percentage of people who felt the government was being run for the benefit of all imploded from 64% in the 1960s to just 19% today, and the percentage of the population who believed the government was being run for a few big powerful interests soared from 27% in the 1960s to an astonishing 79% today. In a Europe-wide poll, when asked, 'Do you believe politicians care about you or your concerns,' 63% of those surveyed in a dozen countries across the continent answered: 'No.'

So we're seeing nothing less than a massive divide

opening up between the people and the political class, and this divide is evident on an international scale. For example, in a survey taken by the Chatham House, a British thinktank, a poll taken around the time of Brexit, when asked if immigration was good for Britain, 60% of British members of parliament answered yes, while only 25% of the public felt the same way.

In light of Chapter One, we can now see that these resentful sentiments of alienation and disenfranchisement were organically forged in the midst of the rise of neo-feudalism: an increasingly meta-capitalist society defined by the concentration of enormous power and affluence in the hands of fewer and fewer people. As it turns out, the profound political and economic divide widening between the people and the political class is the key contradiction that is completely redefining adversely popular political sentiment all throughout the West. And it's not surprising that given how comfortably members of the legacy media fit within the milieu of our cultural elite, they failed miserably in recognizing this seismic political shift, that is until it was too late.

THE CRISIS OF LEGITIMACY AND

DEALIGNMENT: THE RISING TRUMP COALITION

What's vitally important for us to understand in terms of making sense of our turbulent time is that these three dynamics of postnormality—complexity, chaos, and contradiction—are together contributing to a growing trend known as *delegitimization.* Scholars are writing more and more about the fact that our politics are experiencing a profound crisis of legitimacy, where there's a very deep discontent among people both on the left as well as the right who feel completely alienated from our public and cultural institutions. Gallup conducted a recent study which found that Americans' trust and confidence in every single major institution has reached very dangerous lows.[40] Some scholars, such as Anthony Monteiro of Temple University, who is a leftwing activist and academic, argue that the United States may indeed be the single most divided country in the world.

Yet, what is crucial to understand is how this growing gap, this widening alienation between the people and our ruling elite, is key to Trump's growing coalition.

---

[40] Jeffrey M. Jones, "Confidence in U.S. Institutions Down; Average at New Low," Gallup, February 7, 2024.

Delegitimization is contributing to what Goodwin and Eatwell refer to as *dealignment,* a breakdown of the bonds that used to exist between traditional political parties and their constituents, and this breakdown in the bonds that voters have had with traditional parties is making it easier for new political challengers to rise up and take the nation in a new direction.

For example, in Britain, back in the 1960s. Around 50% of the population felt strongly aligned to one of the two traditional parties, the Tories or Labour. By 2015, that loyalty had collapsed to just 13%. And when you look at the Brexit issue, support for Brexit cut directly across the traditional party electorates and created an extraordinarily difficult situation, particularly for Labour politicians! Most of Labour's constituents, who were historically working class voters, supported Brexit, while their Labour representatives overwhelmingly opposed it.

And so, in the last national election in Britain, back in December of 2019, those working-class voters defected and voted overwhelmingly Conservative, many for the very first time in their whole lives, giving the Conservatives their largest landslide victory in nearly a century!

In 2016, Trump's support betrayed precisely this kind of dealignment. Nearly 200 counties in Ohio, Wisconsin, Iowa, Michigan, and Pennsylvania that had voted Democrat in every presidential election since the 1980s, including counties that had voted for Barak Obama twice, suddenly voted for Donald Trump, some by as much as a 15% margin. In comparison to the previous presidential election in 2012, Trump got 180,000 more votes in Ohio than Romney, 165,000 more votes in Michigan, and an astounding 290,000 more votes in Pennsylvania.

Similarly, as the poll data accumulates for 2024, Trump's support continues to reveal precisely this kind of dealignment fueled by delegitimation. Trump is currently galvanizing the rural white vote like he did in 2016 and 2020, but at the same time, he's also galvanizing a larger share of the urban non-white vote than any Republican presidential candidate has been able to do in half a century, since Richard Nixon.

And the question, again, is why? Why is Trump attracting so many non-white voters who normally vote Democrat?

MSNBC, of all places, recently did a report on black

voters in Georgia who are supporting Trump, and the voters they interviewed all said that they knew dozens of fellow blacks who always voted Democrat who are now voting for Trump because they believe that Trump is being victimized by the same rigged judicial system that so many of them believe they've been victimized by. And ironically, it's the same with rural voters; we have a number of studies, such as J.D. Vance's *Hillbilly Elegy*, that show that rural voters feel completely disenfranchised and shut out from the political and justice systems in the nation comparable to the way urban non-white voters feel.

So this is the irony of all of the neo-feudalized lawfare Democrats have inflicted into the 2024 campaign: it's actually making Trump stronger! The weaponized legalism of indictments and convictions has put Trump ironically in a political sweet sport: he's maximizing the rural white vote for himself all the while minimizing the urban non-white vote for Biden, as both constituents continue to lose confidence in the very public institutions that Democrats have largely attempted to weaponize.

SUMMARY

We can now see how the rise of neo-feudalism, by its own rejection of the very liberalism its proponents claim to uphold, has brought an end to an era and inadvertently ushered in an interim period known as postnormal times. Again, as we saw in Chapter One, I think it is essential for us to recognize that this post-normality was itself initiated by virtue of the destruction of liberalism at the hands of liberals themselves and is hardly the fault of the MAGA loyalists that the legacy media so often disparages as a danger to democracy. This post-normative period is characterized by three main processes–complexity, chaos, and contradiction–that are all dramatically disruptive of previous liberal norms:

- Complexity is characterized by competing nationalisms based on different conceptions of identity.

- Chaos is fomented by hyper-connective communication networks that have completely disrupted the liberal media's monopoly on information dissemination.

- Contradictions increase as the power and wealth

discrepancies between the haves and have-nots continue to widen and expand.

The cumulative effect of these three postnormal dynamics is:

1. A legitimation crisis surrounding our liberal institutions

2. An increasing dealignment among voters from traditional politics and parties, thus opening up unprecedented opportunities for new politicians to take politics in new directions. It is precisely these processes, ironically ushered in by the crisis of liberalism provoked by liberals themselves, that are propelling the Trump phenomenon; hence why I believe Trump is truly our first postnormal president.

The question now is: what is this new politics that's emerging from delegitimation and dealignment? In our comparison between the Brexit vote and the Trump vote in 2016, it appears that common constituencies such as the white working class are voting in similar ways for candidates saying similar things. The irony is that despite the prevailing complexities, chaos, and contradictions in our postnormal time, what's so interesting and frankly unexpected is that these rising new politicians—on both sides of the Atlantic—are all strikingly similar in terms of their politics and platforms! The new public figures disrupting American and European politics are often echoing uncannily complementary values, interests, and concerns, awakening a very noticeable and unified solidarity.

But why is that? How can the politics of complexity, chaos, and contradiction evidence so much unity, order, and coherence? That will be the topic of our next chapter.

CHAPTER THREE

TRUMP AND THE RISE OF CIVILIZATIONAL POPULISM

The weekend of June 6 to 9, 2024, represented yet another stunning political earthquake. Voters across the continent went to the polls for the European Parliament elections. Nearly 400 million citizens in twenty-seven countries cast their votes to elect representatives from their respective countries to serve as lawmakers in the Belgian capital of Brussels. When the exit polls were released throughout the night, the European elite were absolutely shellshocked; in nation after nation, the so-called far right surged to heights never seen before in modern European politics.

It all started in the Netherlands. On the first night of

the elections, the nationalist-populist extraordinaire Geert Wilders and the Dutch Freedom Party went from zero seats in the European Parliament to win upwards of 20% of their seats. Then, in Germany, the Alternative for Deutschland crushed the liberal Green Party to become the second most popular party in the nation and the single most popular party in all of eastern Germany. In Italy, Giorgia Meloni's Brothers of Italy swept their elections, garnering 30% of the vote. In Hungary, Victor Orban's Fidesz Party continued to dominate Hungarian politics, winning a commanding 44% of the vote. But the crown jewel of the weekend belongs to Marine Le Pen's National Rally in France, winning over 30% of the vote while delivering a humiliating blow to President Emmanuel Macron's party. Macron responded by dissolving parliament and ordering snap elections.

The rise of National Rally provides an informative snapshot of the astonishing growth of the nationalist right in general throughout the continent. Back in 1999, National Rally (then National Front) won only 5% of the vote; in 2004, they almost hit 10% but took several steps back in 2009, falling to 6%. But something happened in 2014: they surged to nearly 25% of the vote. They repeated those results in 2019, clocking in at 20%! But as June of 2024, National Rally experienced yet another surge: they cracked the thirty percent mark, positioning themselves as potentially France's premiere political party!

Those patterns have repeated themselves over and over again throughout the last two decades. From the rise of the Austrian Freedom Party to the Sweden Democrats, from Vlaams Belang in Belgium to Vox in Spain, populist right parties have been on the ascent, slowly and steadily redefining the European political order.

It was, therefore, rather ironic that Politico called the June elections 'Europe's Trump moment.'[41] Such branding betrays the legacy media's typical short-sightedness. After all, Europe has actually been considerably ahead of the United States when it comes to the rise of nationalist populism or what the media so often belittles as 'far right.' As noted above, nationalist populist parties have been on the rise in Europe since the late

---

[41]Stephan Faris et al., "Europe's Trump Moment Has Arrived," POLITICO, June 6, 2024.

1990s, when the United States was being led by a neo-liberal like Bill Clinton!

THE RISE OF CIVILIZATIONAL POPULISM

But perhaps the moniker of 'Europe's Trump Moment' is not so misleading after all, at least to the extent that Trump is the most visible representative of a common politics emerging on both sides of the Atlantic, what scholars are increasingly calling *civilizational populism.*

The key characteristic of populism is generally seen as a distinctly vertical political antagonism as opposed to a horizontal one. So instead of polarizing politics horizontally, seeing the political animus as between the left vs. the right or liberal vs. conservative, this horizontal antagonism, populism reconfigures that polarization vertically, now the animus is between the people vs the political class, the ruled vs rulers, the ordinary American vs the oligarchy. As we saw in the last chapter, the driving dynamic behind this recalibrated polarization appears to be the very delegitimization that is itself the result of the complexities, chaos, and contradictions constitutive of postnormal times.

However, what's interesting is that populism is generally seen as a very thin ideology in that, as a restructuring of the political animosity, it lacks any definable and thick ideological import. This is why you can have populists on the left and populists on the right, such as the Brothers of Italy and Lega on the populist right and Five Star on the populist left, or in Germany, the AfD on the right and Die Linke on the left. What often happens is that populism gets combined with other beliefs and ideas of politics that provide the particular rationale and justification for the vertical divide; in other words, the thicker political ideology explains *why* the division between the people and the political class is happening.

Academics such as the Israeli scholar Ihsan Yilmaz are calling the dominant populism of our time *civilizational populism,* which categorizes people according to their civilizational identities and asserts the incompatibility of different cultures and religions. Proponents of civilizationalism believe politics should be an expression of the will of the people and that society is ultimately comprised of two antagonistic groups: the people who are the faithful custodians and defenders of civilization versus a corrupt and degenerate elite who collaborate with what Yilmaz calls 'dangerous others' belonging to other civilizations who together represent a clear and present danger to the civilization and way of life of the people. Civilizationalism is thus a discourse that explains the world in terms of clashing civilizations and posits that our civilization is threatened by a foreign invasion (both ethnic as well as ideological) ultimately represented and advocated by a corrupt globalist elite.

POST-SECURITY POLITICS

So, what's driving this civilizational populism? Why is *civilization* providing the thick ideology for the thinness of populism?

Civilizational populism appears to be animated by what Cornell sociologist Mabel Berezin has identified as three *insecurities* that have grown rampant throughout the West over the last decade: insecurities that are provoked by globalized dynamics.[42] Berezin notes that the nation-state historically promised to provide secure borders, a stable economy, and the space for the celebration and perpetuation of a population's customs, traditions, and religion. But as Berezin observes, these three securities have eroded as the result of dynamics inherent in globalization.[43]

First, because the constituents of globalization, such as transnational corporations and electronic money, transcend national borders, many scholars believe that globalization is bringing an end to the whole concept of distinct nations. As Paul Harris has observed, these porous borders, which serve to expedite the flow of goods within a globalized economy, entail a significant increase in levels of immigration, both legal and illegal.[44] Moreover, the threat of terrorism only exaggerates the

---

[42] Mabel Berezin, "The Normalization of the Right in Post-Security Europe," in Armin Schäfer and Wolfgang Streeck (eds.), *Politics in the Age of Austerity* (Cambridge: Polity Press, 2013), 239-61.

[43] Berezin, Mabel. "Globalization Backlash." Cornell, http://people.soc.cornell.edu/mmb39/Forthcoming%20Globalization%20Backlash.pdf.

[44] Harris, Paul A. "Immigration, Globalization and National Security: An Emerging Challenge to the Modern Administrative State." http://unpan1.un.org/intradoc/groups/public/documents/aspa/unpan006351.pdf.

anxieties over the porous borders, rendering border insecurities a seemingly permanent part of our political and national landscapes.

Secondly, globalization tends to negate local industry with a global division of labor that relocates manufacturing to the global South, while finance and ownership of capital have coalesced around the West. As a result, the last few decades have been characterized by a mass exodus of industrial and manufacturing jobs from the U.S. and Western Europe into so-called third-world or global South nations such as Mexico and China. The economic collapse of 2008 hit Europe hard, particularly the young. Net employment in the eurozone fell by about 6 million between 2008 and 2013, and half of those affected were under the age of twenty-five. It's hardly surprising that millennials' confidence in the European Union and economic integration has imploded; for example, in Spain, only about 30% of youth support the EU, while in Italy, it's down to just 12%.

Thirdly, border and economic insecurities are rivaled by ontological or cultural insecurity. One of the consequences of the disembedding dynamics in globalization is what scholars call *detraditionalization*. Once social life is caught up in a global industrialized economic system, it is propelled away from traditional, national, and local practices and beliefs. As a result, traditional moral codes and cultural customs become increasingly implausible to objectively sustain, and populations increasingly sense that the beliefs and practices so central to their historic cultural identity are withering away.

And so, as Berezin concludes, the globalized emergence of these insecurities has provided the political context and climate in which nationalist populist solutions to political issues appear plausible and normal. In Yilmaz's terms, post-security politics provide the constituents that define a populism animated by distinctively civilizationalist concerns. Thus, as the successful Brexit referendum anticipated, the Trump phenomenon is hardly specific to the United States, that is, of course, if we understand that phenomenon as a manifestation of a far wider and deeper emergent politics, a politics that is largely a backlash against the insecurities provoked by globalization.

In what follows, I want to explore how these civilizationalist concerns have already significantly redefined politics on both sides of the Atlantic and how they promise to influence politics inordinately for the foreseeable future.

BORDER SECURITY

Back in January of 2019, Farhad Manjoo of *The New York Times* penned an op-ed entitled: "There's nothing wrong with Open Borders."[45] It was a stunningly brazen piece that made the case for why 'a brave Democrat' should step forward and defend the notion that the United States, far from closing its borders, should, in fact, be vastly expanding our immigration policy to accommodate anyone and everyone who wants to come into our nation. Channeling his inner John Lennon, he writes:

Imagine not just opposing President Trump's wall but also opposing the nation's cruel and expensive immigration and border security apparatus in its entirety. Imagine radically shifting our stance toward outsiders from one of suspicion to one of warm embrace.

---

[45] Farhad Manjoo, "There's Nothing Wrong with Open Borders," The New York Times, January 17, 2019.

Imagine that if you passed a minimal background check, you'd be free to live, work, pay taxes, and die in the United States. Imagine moving from Nigeria to Nebraska as freely as one might move from Massachusetts to Maine.

He went on to challenge Democratic presidential hopefuls, all surfacing at the time, to radically expand our immigration policies. After all, why is it that certain people are afforded certain rights and benefits simply by accident of geography? Why is it that we here in the United States are afforded all of these 'rights' whereas people in other nations, say on the continent of Africa, where he's from, are excluded from enjoying such rights? He actually quotes a professor from the University of Hawaii who claims that closed borders in our modern world represent a new form of feudalism in that our world is predicated on the notion that we are recipients of hereditary rights and privileges based on where we were born.

He further cited selective studies that showed that immigrants are no more prone to violence than your average citizen, that they're not a threat to entry-level employment for citizen workers, and that we need not worry about their propensity towards welfare benefits. He then makes the case that our nation here in the States is aging with a stagnant population, and if we're ever going to compete effectively with India and China, we're going to have to open up our borders.

Ironically, after all that effort, Manjoo admitted that his proposal lacks one key element: *reality.* He recognized that his views were rather far-fetched, realizing that the whole notion of open borders was anathema to most Americans. He acknowledged that even the Democratic Party at the time was largely having to give in to the increased border security rhetoric. He knew a vast majority of Americans wanted a border wall of some kind on our southern border. But he failed to come to terms precisely with *why* so many have turned away from this whole notion of open borders. He seemed content, as most liberal globalists are, to chalk it all up to good 'ol' fashioned' xenophobia and racism, which, of course, turns out to be rather xenophobic and racist on his part, ascribing racist attitudes to a single race is itself racist.

But more to the point, the reason more and more Americans are rejecting open borders is because they are rejecting the very globalism that *The New York Times* stands for. It's not just a matter of the threats in crime and the like; that's been well established. In 2019 year alone, 1.7 million pounds of narcotics were seized at the border. Ninety percent of our heroine comes in through the southern border. In fact, in 2017, enough opioids were seized at the southern border to kill every single man, woman, and child in this nation. In 2018, over 250 thousand illegal immigrants were deported, among which 6,000 were known or suspected gang members; nearly 140,000 illegal immigrants arrested by ICE last year had criminal records; 80,000 were caught drunk driving. Over 50,000 were arrested for violent assaults, and over 2,000 were arrested for murder. In fact, we have statistics that show that illegal aliens are disproportionately more likely to commit murder in our nation than our own citizens. And don't forget that we have what are called 'special interest aliens'; those are illegal aliens that pose a significant threat to the security of our homeland, in other words, potential terrorists. The number of special interest aliens that were caught by border enforcement in 2018 was over 3,000.

But it's far deeper than all of this. You'll notice that

among all the reasons that this opinion columnist listed for why open borders are such a virtue, he left out what is perhaps the single most cited reason for why more and more Americans and Europeans want their borders closed, and that major reason is in a word: culture. As far as globalists like this are concerned, Western culture appears to be radically negligible at best and frankly wicked at worst. His excoriating Americans for being xenophobic actually ignores the fact that studies show that racist attitudes are at an all-time low here in the States as well as in Europe. He also ignores studies such as the one by Harvard scholars Steven Levitsky and Daniel Ziblatt that argue that there is no example in history anywhere of a successful multi-racial democracy where the once-majority group has become a minority.

Unfortunately for our coastal elites, the simple fact of the matter is that for tens of millions of people, culture matters; national and religious identity matters; custom and tradition matters. To brush that all aside as if they were totally irrelevant to the concerns of an increasing number of populations is nothing more than willful ignorance, a deliberate attempt to sequester legitimate democratic concerns from the national debate defined and limited by secular globalist sensibilities. But they do so at their own political and cultural peril. In 2016, we found that in counties that have seen the highest proportion of migration, particularly illegals moving in between the years of 2000 and 2015, those counties that changed most dramatically in terms of an incoming immigrant population were disproportionately more likely to vote for Donald Trump in 2016.

This is the massive backlash against unfettered immigration that we're seeing not just here in the States but indeed throughout the world; that's why 2016 has been called by one publication "Year of the Wall"; it's been called the year of the wall because everywhere you look, nations are tightening their borders. You can look at France, Hungary, India, Austria, Italy, Greece, and Israel; you can go on and on and on and on. Everywhere we look, border walls are going up; they're not coming down. And why are they going up? It's largely because massive immigration has, in fact, begun to change their nation, culture, customs, and tradition in ways that have simply rendered their nation unrecognizable. As we see with this *New York Times* article, globalists could care less; globalists don't care about nation, culture, custom, and tradition; they don't care about the rights of majority groups; and they don't care about the fact that there's never been a successful democracy where the majority demographic became a minority. They just don't care.

But Americans and Europeans increasingly do. Virtually every poll taken over the last decade shows that the vast majority of the nation wants strict border security and that support cuts across all partisan allegiances. For example, in a Harvard/Harris poll taken just last year that sampled nearly 2,000 registered voters, 75% of respondents said they would be more likely to support a candidate who supported strict border security.[46] Interestingly, that included 75% of black registered voters, one of the Democrats' most loyal constituencies. More recently, a CBS poll found that 62% of respondents supported the deportation of *all* illegal migrants. While CBS news anchors were noticeably shocked by the poll results, what escaped their surprise was the fact that this 2024 poll was virtually identical to a previous poll

---

[46] John Binder, "Poll: 3-in-4 Voters Favor 'America First' Immigration, Trade, War Platform," Breitbart, March 3, 2019.

taken by CBS four years earlier, which showed that over 60% of Americans want immigrants illegally coming over the border arrested and deported.[47] Only 20% said they should be allowed to stay.

Such sentiments are hardly specific to the United States. A 2017 Ipsos Mori poll that surveyed nearly 18,000 voters in twenty-five countries in Europe found that 43% of British, 54% of Hungarians, and 63% of Italians believed that quote "immigration is causing my country to change in ways that I do not like." There was also a recent poll taken by YouGov that asked voters across Europe what their top two political priorities were, and the answer was the same in every single state: immigration and terrorism.

It's no wonder that Joe Biden's southern border fiasco is consistently one of his most unpopular policies. A Monmouth poll recently had Biden's approval tanking to the low twenties when it came to his handling of immigration on the southern border. Even Democrat loyalists like New York Mayor Eric Adams have excoriated

---

[47] Ariel Zilber, "CBS' Margaret Brennan Shocked That Most Americans Back Deporting Illegal Immigrants," New York Post, June 10, 2024.

Biden's handling of the southern border. At the time of this writing, 50% of New York's hotel capacity is being taken up by hundreds of thousands of illegal migrants bussed into New York from Texas due to the political brilliance of Texas Governor Greg Abbott.[48] Adams was so desperate to stop the inflow of illegal migrants into his city that he signed an executive order that would impound the buses of drivers caught bussing migrants into New York.

The contrast with Trump's border security policies simply could not be starker. According to data from US Customs and Border Protection, President Trump oversaw the lowest illegal border crossings in nearly fifty years. In 2017, there were 415,517 instances of illegal border crossing, the lowest since 1971. By contrast, in Biden's first two years, there were an estimated 4 million illegal border crossings, an all-time high![49]

It is, therefore, no coincidence that Trump, as part

---

[48] Chris Donaldson, "NYC Mayor Adams Threatens to Impound Buses, Blames Tx Governor as Migrants Keep Rolling In," BizPac Review, December 29, 2023.

[49] (@CloumbiaBugle), "The border crisis ends like when immigration ends. #AmericaFirst", X, Jan 8, 2023.

of his 2024 platform, is promising the single largest deportation operation in American history. Like *The New York Times* call for open borders, Axios couldn't help sounding the alarm over how Trump's plan to crack down on immigration includes using a wide range of tools to deport millions of people from the U.S. every single year of his presidency.[50] Trump's plans reportedly include mobilizing the US military as well as law enforcement officers from all levels of government. Upon election, Trump is planning to mobilize Immigration and Customs Enforcement agents, National Guard troops, and state and local law enforcement officers to carry out the mass deportations.

But what's so important to underscore here is that Trump is simply advocating policies that are consistent with this sentiment of border insecurity so widespread among populations in both the States and Europe. Again, even Axios admitted that 42% of *Democrats* support mass deportations![51] Thirty percent of Democrats sup-

---

[50] Steph W. Kight, Courtenay Brown, and Russell Contreras, "Inside Trump's Plans to Deport Millions from the U.S.," Axios, February 11, 2024.

[51] Margaret Talev and Russell Contreras, "America Warms to Trump's Harshest Immigration Plans," Axios, April 25, 2024.

port ending birthright citizenship, where a baby gets automatic citizenship simply for being born on American soil. According to a Rasmussen survey, 74% of likely voters said the border situation is not merely a crisis; it is, in fact, an invasion, and a whopping 71% approve of more border wall construction; 63% say border security is a vital national security interest and 54% say Trump is right about the wall.[52] And these are all *black voters,* the single most loyal constituency to the Democrat Party!

The key takeaway here is that regardless of what happens in November of 2024, all the data overwhelmingly suggests that the concerns over border security will continue to be a major priority among voters on both sides of the Atlantic for the foreseeable future.

ECONOMIC SECURITY

In 2019, the Dutch government, pressured by the powerful environmentalist movement in Europe, decided to crack down on farm emissions. The new regulations

---

[52] (@Rumussen_Poll), "TODAY - Inflation and illegal immigration top the list of issues voters...", X, May 10, 2024.

forced farmers to use less fertilizer cut their livestock herd numbers (which often involved killing their livestock), or even stop work altogether.

The response was massive and furious. Dutch farmers have brought their cities to a standstill; tractors and trucks have shut down entrances to motorways, bridges, and tunnels, in some cases blocking off entryways to entire cities. These were hardly ideologues. They weren't political left or right, conservative or liberal; they were farmers, and they rose up to defend their livelihood and their unique way of life. The Dutch farmers' revolt sparked an inferno of protest that engulfed the whole continent, with farmers from Germany, France, Italy, Greece, and Spain joining in and assembling ultimately in Brussels, the de facto capital of the European Union.

A number of pundits and scholars are calling it a kind of Trumpification of world politics, a populist revolt against an aloof economic elite.[53] But this revolt is actually an uprising against the wider social discrepancies inherent in globalist economic policies centered on

---

[53] Mariano Aguirre, "Trumpism, an Ideology for the Extreme Far-Right Globally," openDemocracy, December 14, 2020.

what's called a *global division of labor.* This is where manufacturing and industrial factory jobs have been shipped out from the United States and Europe to the global south while capital and finance have been reallocated around urban metropolitan centers in the global north, such as New York, London, and Paris, a process has left rural populations highly unemployed. For example, scholar Christopher Guilluy has pointed to the growth of what he calls 'peripheral France,' which is made up of people who can't live in urban centers because of its gentrification but who also can't necessarily find jobs in the rural areas in which they live; so those who comprise peripheral France feel like they've been completely shut out not just from globalization, but also from the national conversation and decision making.[54] And to make matters even worse, between the years of 2004 and 2013, France spent nearly 40 billion Euros to refurbish and rebuild mainly ethnic-minority housing centers throughout their cities, but they

---

[54] Lara Marlowe, "Twilight of the Elites Review: An Insight into France's Gilets Jaunes," The Irish Times, March 16, 2019.

didn't do anything even remotely like this on similarly depressed areas inhabited by native French citizens.

In the United States, the globalist erosion of our manufacturing base has been frankly devastating, losing some sixty thousand factories in the fifteen years prior to Trump's first term. Reversing this trend was at the heart of Trump's economic nationalism. During the first years of his first term, we witnessed over 200,000 manufacturing jobs return to the US. Manufacturing unemployment fell to less than 3%, the lowest ever recorded. But it wasn't just manufacturing. The Dow Jones gained over eight trillion dollars in value. Taxes were slashed for some 70% of Americans, most of whom will be paying half of what they paid under the Obama years. Under Obama, the economy never grew past 3%; under Trump, it had grown by an average of over 4%. In terms of energy production, the United States became the largest crude oil producer in the world. Trump renegotiated NAFTA, replacing it with the USMCA (US-Mexico-Canada Agreement), and caused China to blink several times when it came to their unfair tariffs.

While the coming of COVID certainly dampened and depressed these achievements, ironically, the virus only ended up increasing concerns about national and economic security. In March of 2020, as the pandemic swept throughout the globe, David Goodhart published an insightful piece on Unherd entitled: 'Farewell free trade, and good riddance.' The gist of the piece is that the spread of the coronavirus 'sealed the deal', as it were when it comes to the death of globalism and the rise of economic nationalism. He noted two horrific consequences of globalism brought out for all to see by the virus: first, we no longer need rats or fleas to spread disease, but now we can do it ourselves through open borders, mass international travel, and supply chains. Secondly, when things do go wrong, we find that we're no longer self-sufficient to deal with the problem since we've outsourced our manufacturing industries to nations in the global south like China, who are deliberately threatening the global north with the possibility of holding back on sanitation masks and vaccines and medicines that they alone produce. In other words, the coronavirus pandemic is the perfect metaphor for the perils of the hyper-connection that is characteristic of globalization.

As a result, Goodhart observed that those who were

once staunch free traders began noticeably converting over to economic nationalism, most notably Florida Senator Marco Rubio. And it appears that the general public has been converted as well. The same Harvard/Harris poll cited above found that when it comes to trade, 65% of voters said they would be more likely to support candidates who wanted to put tariffs on China. Moreover, 70% said they would support a candidate who wanted to replace NAFTA with bilateral trade agreements that protected American manufacturing and industry. It is very clear from this poll that American voters are solidly in the economic nationalist camp.

Trump's astonishing economic record stands in stark contrast to Biden's performance. GDP growth was 1.6% in the first quarter of 2024, down from 3.4% in the fourth quarter of 2023 and 4.9% in the third quarter. We have record-high government spending and borrowing, record-high credit card debt, and housing costs, which are up by 37% since the first quarter of 2020 through the end of 2023. Inflation rose at a 3.8% annual rate in the first quarter of 2024 and 2.9% in March alone, their highest levels in more than two decades.[55]

A recent Suffolk University poll on the economy found that 70% of the population believes that the economy is getting worse, and those same voters trust Trump over Biden with the economy by double-digits! A Marquette poll released around this same time period found that voters trusted Trump to handle the economy better by twenty-four points, fifty-two to twenty-eight!

The European farmer's revolt, the national vulnerabilities exposed during COVID, and the undeniable popularity of Trump's America First policies all suggest that the rise of economic nationalism across the West is hardly a fluke but is indeed the political economics of the foreseeable future.

CULTURAL SECURITY

In April of 2021, the French news magazine Valeurs Actuelles sent shockwaves throughout the nation. Twenty

---

[55] Paul Davidson, "PCE Inflation Accelerates in March. What It Means for Fed Rate Cuts," USA Today, April 26, 2024.

retired generals and upwards of eighty ex-officers and military service personnel published an op-ed warning that France was actually on the brink of civil war.[56] The open letter came on the heels of the fatal stabbing attack of a policewoman in Paris by a Tunisian immigrant, who was shot dead by police. It was but the latest in a string of Islamic terrorist attacks against French citizens over the previous few months, attacks that were causing more and more French citizens to turn towards populist right parties such as National Rally. But this open letter made explicit what appeared to have been the private fears of many: the growing cultural divide due to unfettered immigration from northern Africa and the Middle East was careening France towards a 'racial war,' with the authors warning: "The hour is grave, France is in peril."

It's not coincidental that such an open letter was published mere months after the George Floyd riots here in the States. The mass looting and burning of cities across the country, to the tune of over $2 billion worth

[56] Henry Samuel, "Retired Generals' Warning of Impending 'Civil War' in France Sparks Political Storm," The Telegraph, April 26, 2021.

of damages, was met with shock and derision by the French. President Emmanuel Macron himself declared that his administration would do everything it could to prevent the disease of extreme leftist "woke" culture from gaining a foothold in France, lest French society unravel in a manner comparable to what was happening in the States.[57] French officials began openly denouncing what they considered the pernicious and venomous cultural Marxist ideas coming out of American universities, and the French government even passed strict prohibitions against gender-neutral language from their official communications and education curriculum. French officials have further taken control over religious funding of mosques, and Macron has even doubled down on their national burka ban.[58]

And yet, what France is doing is largely par for the course in what's happening all across the West. The

---

[57] Frances Mulraney, "'Out-of-Control Woke Leftism and Cancel Culture' from the U.S Is a Threat to FRANCE Because It 'Attacks' the Nation's Heritage and Identity, French Politicians and Intellectuals Say," Daily Mail Online, February 9, 2021.

[58] Jason Silverstein, "France Will Still Ban Islamic Face Coverings Even after Making Masks Mandatory," CBS News, May 12, 2020.

anti-cultural dynamics inherent in globalization have elicited what scholars are calling *retraditionalization*, a renewed interest in "traditions of wisdom that have proved their validity through the test of history," or "a longing for spiritual traditions and practices that have stood the test of time, and therefore can be valued as authentic resources for spiritual renewal."[59] With post-security polity as our backdrop, the important point here is that retraditionalization is not limited simply to spiritual renewal or religious revival; it often involves a reconfiguration of political, cultural, and educational norms around pre-modern religious beliefs and practices as a response to the secularizing processes of globalization.[60]

Examples of retraditionalization abound in the West, particularly in Europe:

Shortly after Trump's election, Poland held a Catholic

---

[59] Leif Gunnar Engedal, "*Homo Viator.* The Search for Identity and Authentic Spirituality in a Post-modern Context," in Kirsi Tirri (ed.) *Religion, Spirituality and Identity* (Bern: Peter Lang, 2006), 45-64, 58.

[60] Ivan Varga, "Detraditionalization and Retraditionalization," in Mark Juergensmeyer and Wade Clark Roof (eds.), *Encyclopedia of Global Religion* (Los Angeles: Sage Publications, 2012), 295-98, 297.

mass aired on national television in November of 2016, declaring Jesus Christ as King and Lord over their nation in the presence of Prime Minister Andrzej Duda. Prime Minister Viktor Orban in Hungary is championing the defense of Christian civilization against secular globalization represented by the European Union; Eastern European nations such as Georgia have reintroduced Orthodox Christianity back into their public school curriculum. In Turkey, a number of scholars have noted that both President Erdoğan and his party, the AKP or Justice and Development Party, are interested in transforming the once secular democratic republic into a neo-Anatolian federation of Muslim ethnicities, a transformation that may even involve a revived caliphate.

It should, therefore, be no surprise that though American society continues to exhibit enormous cultural division, such as we've seen in the aftermath of the 2020 race riots, a mass return to America's cultural heritage is equally evident, most especially in the rise of so-called Christian Nationalism. The most comprehensive study of Christian Nationalist sentiments recently comes from the leftwing Public Religion Research Institute.[61] The study asked 5,000 respondents representing all fifty states if they agreed or disagreed with a series of statements:

The U.S. government should declare America a Christian nation.

U.S. laws should be based on Christian values.

If the U.S. moves away from our Christian foundations, we will not have a country anymore.

Being Christian is an important part of being truly American.

God has called Christians to exercise dominion over all areas of American society.

According to the study, 30% of the American public either agreed or strongly agreed with every single one of those propositions. Moreover, a recent University of Maryland study found that 61% of Republicans supported the formal declaration of the United States as a Christian nation.[62] Interestingly, the study found that

---

[61] PRRI Staff, "A Christian Nation? Understanding the Threat of Christian Nationalism to American Democracy and Culture," PRRI, March 2, 2024.

[62] Stella Rouse and Shibley Telhami, "Most Republicans Support Declaring the United States a Christian Nation," Politico, September 21, 2022.

20% of Democrats would like to see America declared a Christian nation as well!

Needless to say, the hyperbolic rhetoric among our secular elite sounding the alarm on a supposedly immanent theocracy often borders on the hysterical. Take, for example, some of these headlines. The often absurd hysterics of Salon are hard to beat; a September 2021 headline read: 'The Satanists are right: Texas' abortion ban is a direct attack on freedom of religion,' with the bi-line: 'The anti-abortion movement can't be separated from the theocratic movement of white evangelicals or white supremacy.' Another headline from the same website read: 'The plot against America: Inside the Christian right plan to remodel the nation,' with the bi-line: 'The Religious right's blueprint for theocratic state laws keeps creeping forward. Is the left ready to fight?' Or this one: 'The Christian nationalist ASSAULT on democracy goes stealth–but the pushback is working.'

As unlikely as it may have seemed some years ago, what appears rather clear behind all of these hysterics is that the alarm over Christian nationalism reached a pinnacle with the rise of Donald Trump, as evidenced by another Salon bi-line: 'For Christian nationalists, Trump's presidency is a gift from God.' Trump made no secret of his defense of conservative Christian values when he first campaigned in 2016. Trump repeatedly promised to appoint strict constitutionalists to the Supreme Court, he openly excoriated Roe v. Wade for unnecessarily dividing and polarizing our nation, and he promised that Christianity would once again be celebrated in America rather than derided. And the so-called Christian Right reciprocated; in 2016, they made up over 30% of the voting electorate. According to the Pew Research organization, white evangelical Christians voted for Trump by an utterly overwhelming margin, 81% to Clinton's 16%. And Catholic voters, too, supported Trump over Clinton by a twenty-three-point margin, 60% to 37%.

It didn't take long for the legacy media to begin to panic over Trump's promised cultural revolution. Shortly after Trump's inauguration, NBC News reported on what they called a 'snowballing' in state legislatures adopting supposedly 'anti-LGBT adoption bills' aimed at protecting religious organizations from being forced to allow children to be adopted by gay couples.[63] Anticipating the Supreme Court's overturning of Roe v. Wade in June of 2022, the Fulcrum accused the now Trump-packed court of 'marching towards theocracy.'[64] And far-left organizations even set up a website called 'Blitzwatch' (named after Project Blitz, a coalition of pro-traditionalist Christian groups) so as to detail the progress of the Christian right's supposed takeover of the nation and how to mobilize and fight back.[65]

Unfortunately for left-wing activists, whatever mobilized resistance the left can muster appears rather futile. As we saw in Chapter One, this is largely because the left has destroyed the very political liberalism that uniquely imposed the very wall between church and state they so adamantly defend. The era of liberalism is largely over, and with it, the peculiar social arrangements specific to liberalism, such as the absolute division between religion and politics, are fading away as well.

---

[63] Julie Moreau, "Anti-LGBTQ Adoption Bills 'snowballing' in State Legislatures, Rights Group Says," NBC News, April 4, 2019.

[64] Lawrence Goldstone, "Courting Theocracy," The Fulcrum, May 27, 2022.

[65] Blitz Staff, "Project Blitz: The Christian Nationalist Attack on America," BlitzWatch, n.d., accessed July 9, 2024.

POST-SECURITY POLITICS AND THE CHANGING POLITICAL MAP

Post-security politics may already be decisively reshaping our nation. A recent study published by Issues and Insights found that as of March 2024, nearly four million Americans fled counties that voted for Biden in November of 2020.[66] According to the Census Bureau's 'net domestic migration' data, the ten counties that gained the most population through net migration all voted for Donald Trump in 2020. By contrast, all ten counties that saw the biggest negative net migration all voted for Biden. The study found that, overall, people have been fleeing liberal counties in droves ever since Biden was elected. What's key here is that 'leftugees' are not merely fleeing deep blue *states* like California, Illinois, and New York, all of whom are most certainly hemorrhaging population; it's that deep blue *counties* are seeing a massive exodus of residents as well.

Of the 555 counties that voted for Biden, 343 (or 62%)

---

[66] I & I Editorial Board, "The Great Divorce: 3.7 Million Have Fled Counties That Voted For Biden," Issues & Insights, March 25, 2024.

lost population since 2020. Of the 2,589 counties that voted for Trump, 1,726 (or 67%) gained population during the same time period. But what was even more fascinating is that the study found that Trump counties inside blue states saw gains in population, all the while Biden counties inside red states saw declines! For example, in Texas, fifteen of the twenty-two counties that voted for Biden lost population from 2020 to 2023. In Tennessee, while the state gained in population due largely to leftugees, three counties suffered a negative net migration since Biden took office, and all three of those counties voted for Biden (Davidson, Haywood, and Shelby). In Ohio, the six counties with the biggest population losses all voted for Biden. In solid blue New Jersey, only nine of the state's twenty-one counties saw a net gain in population. And six of those nine voted for Trump.

If trends continue, it won't merely be a matter of red *states* getting redder but rather red *counties* getting deeper red. That said, red states are clearly the major beneficiaries of this mass exodus. From 2021 to 2022, an astonishing 46 million people moved to a new zip code, the highest annual total on record, and the vast majority moved from blue states to red states.[67] Today, red states have more people in residence to work than before the pandemic. Tennessee enjoyed the fastest growth of any state, followed by Florida and Texas.

And it's not just residents that have been leaving; it's companies. Tesla has left California for Texas, hedge-fund titan Citadel has left Illinois for Florida, and blue-collar Caterpillar is decamping to Texas. Even Seattle-bred Amazon now splits its headquarters between Virginia and Tennessee. All told, investment in new manufacturing facilities throughout red states is up an astonishing 116% in the last year alone.[68] And to crown it all off, the Legend Tower, which is set to be the new tallest building in the nation at 1,907 feet, is being built in the heart of red state America: Oklahoma City.

SUMMARY

As this wide-ranging survey demonstrates, post-security

---

[67] Michael Hendrix, "The Numbers Are in: Red States Are Winning," The Spectator World, July 8, 2022.

[68] Awfblog, "Construction of U.S. Manufacturing Facilities Soar by 116 Percent," America's Work Force Union Podcast, September 30, 2022.

concerns and dynamics are recalibrating politics on both sides of the Atlantic in a remarkably similar way. From the back-to-back victories of Brexit and Trump in 2016 to the rise of the so-called far-right in Europe in 2024, border security, economic security, and cultural security have emerged as the most common political priorities among voters across the West. These issues of national, economic, and cultural sovereignty have come together to comprehensively forge distinctively civilizational concerns that are providing the particular rationale and justification for the vertical divide between the people and the permanent political class. Given that this tendency towards civilizationalism arises from the insecurities provoked by globalization itself, post-security concerns promise to continue to exercise inordinate influence over the politics of the United States and Europe for the foreseeable future. As such, the rise of the Trump phenomenon appears far more than a mere temporary inconvenience for secular liberals; instead, it is an indelible part of the politics of the future.

CHAPTER 4

TRUMP AND THE RISING MULTIPOLAR WORLD

The scenes coming from Kabul on August 15th, 2021, stunned the world. As American troops withdrew from Afghanistan, the Taliban launched a stunning nation-wide blitzkrieg, seizing the capital city of Kabul in mere days. Scenes of tens of thousands of Afghans flooding the Kabul airport, desperate to flee their country, shocked viewers around the globe. The hope of a pro-Western Afghan republic crumbled in the blink of an eye.

Among the numerous commentaries and articles that followed Biden's disastrous troop withdrawal, one stood out; a piece entitled 'The End of American Hegemony.'[69] The article was written by none other than Francis Fukuyama. What followed amounted to nothing short of a self-recusal of his very own 'end of history' thesis he so confidently put forward just a few decades prior.

In the early 90s, after the fall of the Soviet Union, Fukuyama put forward a bold thesis that argued that with the defeat of fascism in World War II, the collapse of communism, and the end of the Cold War, the history of political and social order had evolved finally into the triumph of liberal democracies around the world. As such, the world had finally arrived through this long historical process to discover the single best political and economic system for all peoples around the globe. It was a highly influential thesis among neo-liberals. In many ways, theorists and politicians, echoing Fukuyama, believed that it was the European Union that was the supposed apex of this historical progression, with its combination of democratic institutions, integrated markets, and open borders. This is what Fukuyama now

---

[69] Francis Fukuyama, "Francis Fukuyama on the End of American Hegemony," The Economist, November 8, 2021.

infamously referred to as the 'end of history,' a global liberal democratic order that would usher in an era of peace and prosperity around the world.

Well, as it turns out, Fukuyama later published a piece entitled 'Second Thoughts,' second-guessing the thesis given the nationalist-populist developments since its first

publication.[70] But now, after the fall of Kabul, it appeared Fukuyama was having third thoughts! In an ironic twist, Fukuyama admitted that we are indeed seeing the end of history, but it is the end of the neoliberal era, the demise of the American-led liberal international order. The chief reason such an American-led neoliberal order is cracking up around the globe is precisely because it's cracking up here at home! And that crack-up involves the replacement of liberal *ideology* with post-liberal *identity*. As we explored in Chapter Two, the complexities of a postnormal interim involve competing and contradictory notions of what it means to be an American, and this clash over incommensurate

---

[70] Francis Fukuyama, "Second Thoughts: The End of History 10 Years Later," Wiley Online Library, February 1, 2011.

identities has eroded the political foundation for the liberal globalism that was supposed to bring history to its end.

Obviously, Fukuyama is hardly alone in assessing that the era of Western liberalism is over. In what follows, I want to explore not only how that order is giving way to what scholars are increasingly calling a multipolar order but also how Trump uniquely contributed to the unraveling of the liberal international order.

TRUMP AND THE END OF THE LIBERAL INTERNATIONAL ORDER

The so-called 'liberal international order' can be described as a body of rules, norms, and institutions that govern international affairs. That latter term is key: since World War II, the United States set up a number of institutions, such as the International Monetary Fund, the World Bank, and the World Trade Organization, that established and governed the rules, expectations, and protocols for international relations. After the fall of the Soviet Union in December of 1991, the Soviet bloc of institutions such as the Warsaw Pact and Comecon (The Council for Mutual Economic Assistance) came to an end, and the American-based international order came to full fruition. And because the sole superpower overseeing, protecting, and enforcing this new institutionalized international order was a liberal democracy, the post-Soviet world has since been referred to as the liberal international order.

But as we've thus far seen, order is at the brink, and ironically, America's domestic politics are much to blame for that. As the soon-to-be first postnormal president, Trump actually campaigned on ending the liberal international order. He made no secret of his dislike for the EU and NATO, which he openly called "obsolete," and was an ardent defender and supporter of the Brexit referendum passed in June of 2016.[71] Trump was a harsh critic of the key institutions that comprise the liberal international order, such as the IMF and the World Bank, and made the case for pursuing protectionist economic policies, emphasizing the protection of U.S. workers above all else. In fact, shortly after Trump assumed office, German Chancellor Angela Merkel, a committed

---

[71] Ashley Parker, "Donald Trump Says NATO Is 'Obsolete,' UN Is 'Political Game'," *New York Times*, April 2, 2016.

globalist, warned that Europe could not depend on the United States the way it once did, saying that Europeans "really must take our fate into our own hands."[72]

Trump rejected the globalized propensity towards multilateralism, where multiple countries are lopped together under a single hegemonic international institution such as the WTO. Trump's ire was particularly directed towards China. He overturned a decades-long policy in the West of integrating China into the liberal international order, choosing instead a policy of confrontation and containment. Trump came out and said explicitly that it was a mistake to admit China into the WTO since the protectionist policies of Beijing consistently violated the institution's unilateral rules and protocols.[73]

Trump gutted NAFTA, signed by Bill Clinton back in 1994, and replaced it with the USMCA or the United States-Mexico-Canada-Agreement, a name reflecting

---

[72] Henry Farrell, "Thanks to Trump, Germany Says It Can't Rely on the United States. What Does That Mean?" *Monkey Cage* blog, *Washington Post*, May 28, 2017.

[73] Shawn Donnan, "U.S. Says China WTO Membership Was a Mistake," *Financial Times*, January 19, 2018.

the nationalist tone of the agreement. He imposed tariffs on steel and aluminum imports coming from most countries, including the EU. Trump withdrew from the Trans-Pacific Partnership, halted negotiations with the EU on a Transatlantic Trade and Investment Partnership, and refused to nominate judges to the WTO's appellate body. And in a snub to the worldwide environmentalist movement, he withdrew the US from the Paris Climate Agreement.

However, while Trump was certainly responsible for contributing to the demise of the liberal international order, it would be a grave mistake to think such a demise was specific to Trump's nationalist policies. Geopolitical scholars such as John Mearsheimer have long recognized that this US-based order is cracking due to a number of frailties built into it.[74] America's transformation into a crusader nation, undeterred in its mission to spread liberal democracy around the globe has faced fierce resistance among unwilling populations, poised

---

[74] John J. Mearsheimer, "Bound to Fail: The Rise and Fall of the Liberal International Order," MIT Press Direct, April 1, 2019.

relations with other countries, and has led to a number of deadly and disastrous wars.

Moreover, as we explored in the previous chapter, the globalist dynamics inherent in the liberal international order are provoking a profound security crisis among populations, particularly in the *West*, and that crisis is significant in that it is the collective West that is the supposed custodian of the liberal international order. The porous borders of globalist trade and immigration, along with the rule of unelected multilateral institutions, are not simply clashing with hostile nationalisms abroad; they are clashing with issues of sovereignty and national identity at home, inside the US, and in Europe. As even Fukuyama himself recognized, such domestic strife only serves to undermine the international order as a whole.

THE GREAT RETURN: RETERRITORIALIZATION

As the liberal international order unravels, a fascinating political, economic, and cultural dynamic is emerging throughout the world, a process known as *reterritorialization.* As the term would seem to indicate, it involves a process that is very much the opposite of the disembedding dynamics inherent in globalization.[75] Because globalization is a transnational system, it by its nature disembeds or dislodges political power away from localized control, away from communities and districts and counties, and recalibrates that political power into the hands of a centralized political and economic elite, what is, in effect, a managerial class. This managerial class oversees what globalist scholars call *expert systems*. Given that technocracies, by their nature, operate according to highly complex mechanisms that require fields of expertise to operate effectively, technocracies are generally run by a class of so-called experts who inevitably consolidate power in accordance with their own unique field of expertise: international relations, banking, monetary policy, energy, national security, supply chains, etc. And so, with the unraveling of such a centralized, globalized order, populations are increasingly reterritorializing, taking political power back away

---

[75] Anthony Giddens, *Runaway World: How Globalization is Reshaping our Lives* (New York: Routledge, 2000).

from the hands of transnational elites and reasserting their national, economic, and cultural sovereignty.

In many respects, this process of reterritorialization is the key to understanding the new

post-globalist world that's emerging all around us because it helps to explain the extraordinary diversity and plurality of political orders emerging. This is because, while all populations are currently reterritorializing, they are not reterritorializing in the same way! This multiplicity is, of course, a definitional trait to populations reterritorializing, in that their respective unique cultures will have an inordinate influence on their increasingly localized politics and economics.

That said, reterritorialization appears to be working out around the world in three distinct ways:

1. new nationalist movements

2. new separatist or tribalist movements

3. the rise of civilization states

First, we are seeing the rise of new nationalist

movements all over the world. These are movements that are characterized by a renewed commitment to restoring national sovereignty and a collective reassertion of the nation-state as opposed to the transnationalist forces of liberal globalism. This is what's animating Trump and the MAGA movement in the US, the incredibly successful government of Viktor Orban in Hungary, and the rise of the populist right throughout Europe, such as Marine Le Pen's National Rally, Giorgia Meloni's Brothers of Italy, and Geert Wilders' Dutch Freedom Party.

However, as we explored in Chapter Two, there are at least *two* kinds of nationalism: *civic* and *ethnic*, and that leads us to the second outworking of reterritorialization, which involves separatist or tribalized movements. French sociologist Michel Maffesoli predicted decades ago that a post-modernist society would organically work out into populations increasingly organizing themselves according to racial, regional, and/or religious commonalities.[76] Since the Soviet Union collapsed

---

[76] Michel Maffesoli, *The Time of the Tribes: The Decline of Individualism in Mass Society*. London: Sage, 1996.

in 1991, over thirty-five nations have been added to the world map, many of which resulted from successful secessionist efforts. In Europe, Georgia, Armenia, Belarus, Slovenia, Slovakia, the Czech Republic, Croatia, Bosnia, and Lithuania all found their independence; in Africa, Rwanda, Burundi, and South Sudan; and today, there are a number of major secessionist movements in Scotland, Catalonia, Quebec, and even Texas.

Finally, and perhaps the most titanic expression of reterritorialization, we're seeing the rise of what scholars are calling civilization states, populations that are redrawing their boundaries around ancient civilizational spheres, such as the Slavic Orthodox world of Imperial Russia, the Sino sphere of ancient China, the Hindu nationalist world of Narendra Modi's India.

FROM UNIPOLARITY TO MULTIPOLARITY

The diverse effects of reterritorialization are inevitably pulling the world away from what's often termed a *unipolar order* to a more *multipolar order*. During the years of the Cold War, the world order was characterized by a *bipolar* balance of power between the United States and the Soviet Union. That world, of course, collapsed in December 1991, leaving the United States as the sole superpower on the planet, ushering in a unipolar world and the establishment of the liberal international order.

However, as we've seen in the last decade, that unipolar world has gone through profound changes. With the demise of the liberal international order, a number of great political and economic powers are rising and challenging the United States' hegemony over the globe. China has quickly taken its place as a major world power, and ironically, liberal globalists are largely responsible for it. It was widely believed among Western elites that by getting China hooked on capitalism, as John Mearsheimer describes it, both the Chinese government and the population would get rich and, in the process, reform their ways and become a liberal democratic ally with the US and Western nations. Well, they certainly got rich, and now they're in the process of building a military second-to-none in size and scope. And as for the CCP, it is more powerful and, yes, popular than it has ever been. An example of the enormous scope and power that China has achieved is its shipping industry:

a single Chinese ship plant manufactures more ships than all American ship plants combined!

And then there is the resurrection of Russia. Beginning in 2012, around the time of his third campaign for the presidential office, Vladimir Putin's speeches took a very noticeable civilizational turn.[77] Putin's meta-theme became one involving Russia finding itself in a great civilizational struggle with a decadent, decaying, and dying West. As such, it was imperative for Russia to revive her ancient customs and traditions that have guided the Russian people for a thousand years, so as to defend themselves from the cultural rot that has infested so much of Europe and America. As part of this defense, a renewed Russian civilization would not be merely an inward development, a development happening *inside* a nation; it is also an outward development, in that as more and more nations outside the West experience civilizational renewal, Russia would align itself with those nations to help awaken a new multipolar world.

Trump clearly understands that the world is changing

---

[77] Andrei P. Tsygankov, "Vladimir Putin's Civilizational Turn," Russian Analytical Digest, May 8, 2013.

in ways that the old unipolar perspective could no longer comprehend. He understands that a unipolar world governed by liberal ideology and institutions is giving way to a world reorganized around cultural identity and renewed civilization. As such, he understands that political and economic power no longer revolves around a Western hegemon but is increasingly distributed among various regions around the globe. He appears to recognize that this new multipolar world requires a complementary approach to a more classical balance of power. If a nation is rising too fast, say China, so that its rise starts to become a threat to rival nations like Japan, Australia, and India, then those nations can band together and form an alliance to implement a set of initiatives in order to bring about some regional stability. In a multipolar world, the days of trying to convert China to turning China into an ideological clone of a liberal hegemony are over. Instead, the rising international order of the future is a matter of restoring geopolitical balance specific to multiple regions. The universalistic claims of liberalism and human rights have taken their place on the ash heap of history.

One final note: at the end of the recent Russia-China

summit in Moscow back in March of 2024, President Xi's departing words to Putin were: "Change is coming that hasn't happened in a hundred years, and we are driving this change together."[78] Trump's contribution to the dismantling of the liberal international order was not the ultimate reason for its undoing. As we've seen, a very new world is rising, a world that both shaped and was shaped by Trump. That world will continue to rise regardless of what happens if Trump is reelected or not. All signs indicate that a civilizational, multipolar world, of which Trump and the MAGA movement are very much a part, is, in a word, unstoppable.

---

[78] David Averre, "Xi Jinping Delivers a Chilling Message for the West," Daily Mail Online, March 22, 2023.

CHAPTER 5

TRUMP AND THE PARALLEL ECONOMY

In April of 2023, a video of music icon Kid Rock instantly went viral. But it had nothing to do with music. It was a video of the pop star shooting up a stack of cases of Bud Light in his backyard and then turning to the camera: "F— - Bud Light! F— - Anheuser Busch!"

Why the outrage?

In a word, America's number one selling beer brand, Bud Light, went *woke.* They launched a marketing campaign featuring the trans TikTok star Dylan Mulvaney as their spokesperson. The beer celebrated the '365 Days of Girlhood' milestone that Mulvaney, a biological male, supposedly reached. Given the historic association between Bud Light and traditional working-class values, the sudden embracing of trans activism shocked its loyal consumers. But that shock turned to rage when a video of the vice president of marketing, Allissa Heinerscheid, excoriating and insulting Bud Light's customer base went public.

And it was precisely that outrage that was so forcefully captured in Kid Rock's video.

Needless to say, it was a marketing disaster, one that cost the brand an estimated $1 billion in lost revenue. Indeed, Shark Tank star Kevin O'Leary claimed that the Bud Light disaster would be featured in future marketing textbooks as a case study of what *not* to do as a marketing executive. Once the number-one-selling beer in America, the brand has become synonymous with the most absurd outworkings of woke liberalism.

But Bud Light has actually become a symbol of much more than misguided leftist ideology; in many respects, it has become the emblem of the rise of what scholars call a *parallel economy.* What had gotten largely lost in the midst of the fallout from Bud Light's collapse was that another beer, Ultra Right, positioned itself as a

"100% Woke Free" alternative. It quickly surpassed $1 million in sales, gained over 10,000 customers, and sold over 20,000 six-packs within the first two months of its launch in April of 2023.

These twin dynamics, boycotts, and buycotts, are effectively fueling the rise of an alternative economy where political values are taking center stage in consumer choices. In this chapter, I want to explore how President Trump has been central to the rise of a parallel economy in the United States and how that rise corresponds to the awakening of an even larger international parallel economy that is increasingly providing an alternative to the G-7 and the liberal international order.

CANCELLING A PRESIDENT

On the days of January 7th and 8th, 2021, cancel culture crossed a line no one had imagined possible. Both Twitter and Facebook concurrently suspended the account of the sitting President of the United States. As we saw in Chapter Two and the chaos of our hyperconnected network society, no one in politics had utilized social media like Donald Trump. But all of that changed in the hours following January 6th, 2021, when thousands of protestors stormed the U.S. Capitol building as Congress was in the process of certifying Joe Biden's electors. On Friday of that week, Twitter permanently suspended Trump's account, citing the 'risk of further incitement of violence.' It was the first time any social media outlet had canceled a major world leader.

The suspensions, along with the legacy media's subsequent cheerleading of the bans, were not merely unprecedented; they were audaciously brazen. As we explored in Chapter One, Trump's ban was but the apex of a years-long corporate-state union that formed to deliberately thwart the consent of the governed. As the publishing of the Twitter Files revealed, a public-private partnership emerged between unelected national security bureaucrats in DC together with Big Tech social media outlets that largely bypassed the kind of executive restraints otherwise guaranteed by the very constitutional democracy we were being told such a partnership was protecting. We saw, shockingly, how common it was for ex-FBI agents to find employment at Twitter, and we saw how social media was subject to intense censorship efforts over the course of Trump's presidency. His social media suspension was but the climatic act of these censorship efforts.

THE RISE OF CONSUMER POLITICS

And yet, to the shock of these bureaucratic and billionaire elites, the cancellation of Trump only seemed to awaken yet another mass backlash, this time in the form of *consumer politics.*

Consumer politics involves customers intentionally buying from companies that promote and support their political and cultural values, all the while refusing to purchase from those companies that actively oppose and offend those political and cultural values. Consumer politics involves the twin dynamics we saw above with Bud Light: *boycotts* and *buycotts.* Boycotts are the refusal to purchase from companies that offend one's political and cultural values, while buycotts are intentional purchases from companies that support one's political and cultural values.

A key historical fixed point for the awakening of these twin dynamics and the subsequent rise of the parallel economy was the cancellation of President Trump from

Twitter and Facebook, along with the banning of Parler from AWS, the Apple App Store, and Google Play Store. Such cancellations served as the catalyst for a massive exodus of users away from traditional Big Tech, as well as for a slew of investors pumping money into new tech companies like Rumble and President Trump's own Truth Social, with an entire parallel economy emerging around this nascent communicative network alternative.

Today, virtually any product or service can be found deliberately marketed as a buycott within a parallel economy. Take, for example, Jeremy's Razors. One would think it practically impossible to politicize razors, but astonishingly, Gillette did just that! In January 2019, Gillette released a two-minute commercial that accused men of what is fashionably called today 'toxic masculinity.' Shamelessly pandering to the MeToo movement, the ad featured every pejorative male stereotype imaginable, asking rhetorically: "Is *this* the best a man can get?" Needless to say, the commercial becomes the object of utter scorn and ridicule. But it also occasioned the rise of Jeremy's Razors. One of their ads reads: "Friends don't let friends shave with woke razors. We can't build the parallel economy overnight–it's going to take time. But with your commitment, it will happen. And razors are just the start."

As it turns out, razors are just the start. The conservative Daily Wire is reportedly pouring $100 million dollars as we speak into kid's entertainment in direct response to Disney going woke.[79] The billionaire Peter Thiel is pumping a massive amount of funds into the parallel economy with a FemTech company called '28' that unabashedly affirms the biological reality of what it means to be a woman, and he's the chief investor in Rumble, which has just partnered with the

brand-new payment processor called, conveniently enough, Parallel Economy. Donald Trump Jr. has been on the frontlines of investing in companies like PublicSq, a directory of tens of thousands of conservative companies. And there's now even a parallel jobs site for the non-woke called Red Balloon.

However, few foresaw the explosive impact that Elon Musk's purchase of Twitter for $44 billion would have on this growing alternative economy. Ironically, Musk's

---

[79] Sara Fischer, "The Daily Wire Says It's Pouring $100 Million into Kids Entertainment," Axios, March 30, 2022.

mission to preserve civilization involved restoring free speech to the very social media platform—the largest instant messaging platform in the world—that banned President Trump in the first place! Musk quickly reinstated Trump to the platform (though Trump has yet to tweet, given his commitment to Truth Social), and a number of other influencers were banned around the same time, like Alex Jones. Twitter, or X, as it is now known, has since been central in a worldwide digital network system of instantaneous information, bypassing the censorial gatekeeping of the legacy media and opening up the public square to a number of voices previously silenced by the woke sensibilities of Silicon Valley.

Musk has also been on the frontlines of promoting defi (decentralized finance) and the rise of alt-currencies, specifically cryptocurrencies like Bitcoin and Dogecoin. The world of crypto is increasingly internationally recognized as comprised of viable currencies that are, of course, independent from any particular government, state, or corporation and thus provide an effective hedge against the pernicious practice of debanking. However, cryptocurrencies are actually a leading indicator of an entirely parallel internet technology known as *blockchain*, which promises to eventually replace the current web infrastructure. Economist George Gilder has recently argued that all of these neo-feudalized attempts by Big Tech to silence dissenting voices will soon become irrelevant because we are entering into what he calls a 'post-Google age.'[80] A post-Google age is comprised of blockchain technology that effectively privatizes ownership over one's social media activity. The cryptocosm, by its nature, decentralizes social media control away from Big Tech corporations and disperses ownership to individual users, thus completely disrupting and overturning the current internet infrastructure.

And it's not just a completely alternative internet; even entire institutions are currently being paralleled. With the advent of the pandemic and critical race theory in the classroom, the parallel economy exploded in the

[80] George Gilder, *Life After Google The Fall of Big Data and the Rise of the Blockchain Economy* (Regnery Publishing, 2018).

area of education, particularly in the massive rise in homeschooling.[81]

According to the Home School Legal Defense Association, the number of homeschooled students increased by more than 500% in 2020.[82] In the state of Vermont, for example, homeschooling applications rose by 75% from the previous year. In Nebraska, filings were up 21%!

According to the Association of Classical Christian Schools' membership statistics, there were just ten classical schools in the nation in 1994; today, that number has shot up to over 500.[83] We're also seeing among Catholic schools a mass shift towards rediscovering anew the ancient or traditional way of approaching education. A recent example involves an entire diocese of schools in Michigan that have rejected Common Core by returning to a distinctively Catholic liberal arts education. Moreover, we're seeing the development of

---

[81] NC Family Staff, "A Pandemic's Homeschooling Surge," NC Family Policy Council, December 22, 2020.

[82] Michael P. Donnelly, "Polls Suggest Coronavirus Shutdowns Could Mean Millions More Homeschoolers," The Federalist, May 22, 2020.

[83] ACCS Staff, "The ACCS Our History," Association of Classical Christian Schools (ACCS), March 22, 2023.

networks and organizations such as the Institute for Catholic Liberal Education and annual conferences that are providing the professional development necessary for a vibrant faculty and administration. The charter school movement as well, now representing 10% of publicly funded schools, is becoming fertile ground for classical education. The Great Hearts Academies currently operates twenty-five public charter schools in Arizona and Texas, which together enroll 13,000 students with another 13,000 on waiting lists. The Barney Initiative of Hillsdale College has the second-largest network of public classical schools, serving over six thousand students spanning seven states.

Altogether, the total number of classical charter schools may be upwards of 150 in the nation.

More recently, even the World Economic Forum has found itself faced with a peer competitor. As we saw in Chapter One, the World Economic Forum, founded by Klaus Schwab, is the leading international proponent of stakeholder capitalism, which has effectively merged billionaire and bureaucrat into a neo-feudalized social structure predominant in the United States in particular and Western European nations in general. Each year, representatives from multinational corporations, governments, and civil society organizations, such as George Soros' Open Society Foundations, gather at the luxury resort town of Davos, Switzerland, to propose and impose economic and social policies that effectively recalibrate consumer habits in accordance with the WEF's political and environmental goals.

However, the WEF's top-down technocratic governance was recently challenged by a parallel organization. In late 2023, the city of London hosted the first conference of the Alliance for Responsible Citizenship, or ARC. Over 1,500 attendees from around the world gathered to hear speakers such as the renowned Canadian psychologist and free speech advocate Jordan Peterson, who invited world leaders and businesses to re-imagine the future apart from the apocalyptic and technocratic tyranny that dominates WEF policies. In contrast to the environmental apocalypticism of Davos, ARC advocates a powerful, vibrant, and optimistic vision of human flourishing, foregrounding the importance of religious faith, family values, and freedom of expression for economic development and thriving.

A PARALLEL WORLD

But it's not just the WEF that's getting a peer competitor; it's the whole of the liberal international order. Given the massive civilizational trends we explored in the previous chapter, parallel economies are quite literally springing up all over the planet. For example, UnionPay is China's alternative to Mastercard and Visa and is now actually bigger than Mastercard and Visa.

UnionPay has just cornered over 40% of the world market, surpassing both Visa (38%) and Mastercard (21%). And then there's CIPS, the

Cross-border Interbank Payment System. This is China's substitute for SWIFT, the Society for Worldwide Interbank Financial Telecommunications, which has until recently been the default worldwide financial transaction system. SWIFT was weaponized against Russia by the Biden administration immediately following the Russian invasion of Ukraine in February of 2022, and yet, though Russian banks were largely banned from using SWIFT, the Russian economy remained largely unaffected. This is because Russia simply turned around and recalibrated its economy around the parallel structure of CIPS! So Russia's economy, today, by all measures, is actually booming, even though they just surpassed Iran as the single most sanctioned nation on the planet.

For right or for wrong, that's the power of a parallel economy!

However, parallel economy par excellence is the alternative international economic bloc known as BRICS. In 2006, the nations of Brazil, Russia, India, and China founded the 'BRIC' group, an alliance of the largest developing economies in the world to challenge the political and economic power of the wealthier North American and Western European nations, represented by the G-7. South Africa later joined in 2010, making the group 'BRICS'.

The alliance grew again in August of 2023 when six new nations—Saudi Arabia, Egypt, the UAE, Iran, Ethiopia, and Argentina—were admitted as members (Argentina has since rejected membership with the recent election of Javier Milei as president). Literally overnight, BRICS transformed into the largest economic and political bloc on the planet. The global

GDP-purchasing power parity of the new BRICS+

is now larger than the G7, controlling nearly 40% of the world's GDP and encompassing nearly 50% of the world's population. With the inclusion of three OPEC nations (Saudi Arabia, Iran, and the UAE), the economic block now controls 39% of global oil exports, 46% of proven reserves, and 48% of all oil produced globally! One in every two barrels of oil produced on the planet comes from a BRICS+ member nation! Russia and Saudi Arabia alone account for a quarter of the world's oil production, and Russia and Iran hold the world's first and second-largest gas reserves in the world. Simply put, BRICS+ represents an economic and commodity dominance that was not even imaginable mere months ago!

This is the parallel economy, or better, these are the parallel economies that are rising all over the world. And they're rising up all over the world because, as Chinese President Xi told Russian President Vladimir Putin as they parted from their recent summit, the world is going through the single most epic paradigm shift we've seen in a century. You see, the parallel economy goes way beyond beer alternatives to Bud Light or parallel payment processors. The parallel economy isn't just alternative products and services; *the parallel economy is quite literally a parallel world.* It's a world where the liberal international order is giving way to the rise of civilization states and multipolarity, where political liberalism is giving way to the nationalist, populist, and traditionalist sentiments of post-security politics, and where liberal norms are giving way to the complexities, chaos, and contradictions comprising postnormal times.

And standing at the center of all of these dynamics is, of course, Donald J. Trump. As we have seen, Trump and the MAGA movement are indeed changing not just the United States but much of the wider world as well. But we can now also see how that changing world–that postnormal, post-secure, and parallel world–is, in turn, shaping and influencing Trump and the MAGA movement. I believe this reciprocity is key to understanding not merely the rise of Trump and MAGA but why Trump and MAGA are, in many ways, just the beginning.

CONCLUSION

As I write, the Democrats are doing everything they can to hold on to their crumbling world. A disastrous debate performance by Joe Biden has put his campaign on life-support and panicked political operatives are desperately trying to find an alternative whose name doesn't begin with Kamala. Moreover, after actively campaigning for and championing Joe Biden, whatever trust and confidence the legacy media had left among the electorate completely eroded.

The contrast between Donald Trump and the MAGA movement simply could not possibly be starker. And no, I'm not talking about the polls. I'm talking instead of the massive political, economic, and cultural paradigm shift that is happening all over the world, at the center of which Trump and the MAGA movement are firmly situated. In the previous chapters, we saw precisely how Trump and the MAGA movement are at the forefront of the various dynamics propelling this global tectonic shift:

Trump and the MAGA movement have embraced the nationalist identity politics that are increasingly eclipsing the ideological politics that were so central to the 20th century.

Trump himself uniquely tapped into the power of social media, amassing the largest Twitter handle in the world, while a growing pro-Trump media ecosphere dominated the rising network society, both of which effectively bypassed the legacy media's previous monopoly over news and information.

Trump and the MAGA movement coalesced around the growing populist sentiments that have been redefining the political divide from a horizontal animosity (left vs. right) to a vertical animosity (the people vs. the political class).

Trump and the MAGA movement largely reoriented the Republican Party away from the pro-unipolar, pro-globalist neocon policies of the Bush era toward the border, economic, and cultural issues indicative of the post-security sentiments that are increasingly dominating elections on both sides of the Atlantic.

Trump campaigned on ending the liberal international order and governed accordingly, helping to usher in a more civilizational multi-polar world.

Trump and the MAGA movement have been at the forefront of the burgeoning parallel economy, which, in its international form, is increasingly giving rise to a parallel world, one that is, in turn, hastening the end of the liberal international order.

No other public figure has played such a central role in each of these dynamics—dynamics that show no sign of dissipating. Indeed, the opposite is the case. Politicians are doubling down on identity politics; the network society continues to grow in an increasingly hyperconnected world; the gap between the have's and the have not's is only increasing; populism is on the rise throughout the West; border security, economic security, and cultural security continue to redefine politics on both sides of the Atlantic; the economic and militaristic rise of China, Russia, and India have already effectively eclipsed a unipolar world; and consumer politics promise to continue to polarize our economy, all as the BRICS+ economic bloc continues to attract more and more prospective member nations.

All of this is to say that no matter what happens in November, this astonishing paradigm shift will continue, with or without a cooperative Washington, DC. Our billionaires and bureaucrats remain at the epicenter of what's left of the shattered visage of liberal globalism, demolished by the very tyrannical and irrational impulses that have always been at the heart of political liberalism.

On the other hand, Trump and the MAGA movement are at the forefront of a new and rising world, a world characterized by nationalism, populism, traditionalism, and civilizationalism. It is a world that is facing enormous resistance from globalist powers long entrenched in political power. But that resistance appears to be cracking. Its end is near.

For those who are desperately trying to stop Donald Trump and the rise of MAGA, the news is grim: it's too late. They simply can't be stopped.

Trump and the MAGA movement are indeed changing the world.

***

As the harrowing evening of July 13th came to a close, my wife and I kissed our daughter goodnight and, emotionally drained, we decided to catch a cab back to our hotel. We flagged down a random taxi in the heart of Manhattan, where registered Democrats far outnumber Republicans, and were greeted by the warm smile of our driver. He was a Sikh fellow, born and raised in the Punjab region of India, as I was to later learn. He welcomed us into his cab and we weren't 30 seconds into the cab ride before he asked if we heard about what happened to President Trump. We of course remarked on how shocking and tragic it was for our nation.

But it's what this cab driver said next that shocked us:

"I thank God Almighty for sparing Donald Trump because we need him now more than ever!"

What struck me was that he didn't just say that, again, in a town where Democrats far outnumber Republicans; he said it with so much confidence and boldness! He showed no hesitation, no concern whatsoever for whether we might be easily-triggered liberals.

And then, as if my wife and I weren't blown away enough, he kept going!

"I *love* Donald Trump! I believe he is the true leader of this great and wonderful nation, and I am so thankful God protected him this day!"

And my wife and I were almost in tears. We shared with him how much we, too, loved Trump, how I got to meet him at Mar-a-Lago some months back, and how, yes, we truly believed God intervened for the whole world to see.

But then, it's what he said next that finally brought it all home for me:

"Did you see the people there at that rally? Did you see all those patriots, surrounding him, ducking down to avoid the bullets? They didn't know how many shooters there were, they didn't know anything; all they could do was hear the shots and watch Trump fall." And he said: "Any other crowd would have run in panic! They would have stampeded all over each other to get out of the way! But NOT THAT CROWD! NOT A TRUMP CROWD! They stood their ground! Those people, those brave patriots, they stood their ground!"

As was he. As are tens of millions of patriots all over the world.

They are standing their ground for a new and better world, a good world, a world worth fighting for.

Join a Community of Conservatives, Like No Other

Ever wondered, "What can I do to make a difference?" Since launching my podcast in 2016, I've heard this question countless times. That's why I founded the Courageous Conservatives Club—a dynamic community designed to help you rise above today's challenges and be transformed into a bold, courageous conservative. This is YOUR community!

Join a network of steadfast conservative patriots who uplift and support one another, instead of going at it alone.

As a member, you'll also have the opportunity to get additional exclusive training and courses and be empowered with the skills needed to instill confidence, foster optimism, and restore balance in your life, family, and community during these tumultuous times.

Reignite Our Founding Values

Sign the Declaration of Restoration!

It's time to take a stand. Just like our Founding Fathers, we're facing a critical moment where we must decide–will we fight to restore our nation's values or will we stand by as they're stripped away?

Every day, it feels like we're losing more of what made this country great—our liberties, our faith, our families. But here's the truth: it's not your fault. The Left has been relentless in pushing their agenda, making you feel powerless and isolated. But gang, we don't have to accept this. Just like our Founding Fathers in 1776, we have a choice to make. Will we be the generation that restores liberty and justice, that upholds the values that built this nation?

By signing the Declaration of Restoration and subscribing to Turley Talks, you're joining a community of like-minded patriots who are ready to take action. You'll get the tools you need to stand up boldly—daily insights, exclusive live training with Dr. Steve, and more. This isn't just a subscription; it's a commitment to fight for our freedom and our future.

Subscribe to Turley Talks
and let's take this stand together.
Our time is now.

watch.turleytalks.com/subscribe

Printed in the USA
CPSIA information can be obtained
at www.ICGtesting.com
LVHW072034111024
793587LV00019B/500